Interior Designing for All Five Senses

Interior Designing for All Five Senses

CATHERINE BAILLY DUNNE

with Mary Sears

Photographs by Mark Lohman

St. Martin's Press   New York

www.stmartins.com

Library of Congress Cataloging-in-Publication Data

Bailly Dunne, Catherine.
    Interior designing for all five senses / Catherine Bailly Dunne with
Mary Sears : photographs by Mark Lohman.
        p.   cm.
    ISBN 0-307-44069-9
    1. Interior decoration. I. Sears, Mary. II. Lohman, Mark. III. Title.
NK2110.B28   1998
747—dc21   98-17153
                                                 CIP

First published in the United States by Golden Books

First St. Martin's Press Edition: July 2001

10 9 8 7 6 5 4 3 2

To my beloved husband, James, and
our girls, Kaitlyn and Alexis

—

Acknowledgments

Collaboration is the joy of life—with nature, in my family, in my work, and in my spiritual life.

I have been preparing to write this book my whole life, and I have been so blessed to collaborate with individuals along my journey who have extraordinary vision, wisdom, and energy.

Two people are a part of every page of this book. Mark Lohman is much more than a photographer; he truly is an Artist. It was such a joy to work with someone who not only loved and respected his work, but also demanded the highest levels of excellence from himself.

I'll always treasure my 6:00 A.M. phone calls with Mary Sears. She kept me focused, organized, and most important, laughing! Mary is bright, talented, and inventive. Her creative writing made an enormous contribution to the book.

Also, thanks to Pip Bloomfield and Leelee Durkee, who were invaluable in the day-to-day running of my interior design company and creatively contributed their ideas and talents to this labor of love.

In addition, Robin Tucker is an extraordinary photography stylist, whose patience and artistry flow through the pages of this book. To my brilliant and caring attorney, Alvin Deutsch; Billy Costigan, for his much-appreciated contribution; and Deborah Durham, Steve Smooke, and Missy Denja, for their vivacity and faith.

I'm indebted to many talented individuals who helped bring this book to fruition: Joe Standart, Gabrielle Brooks, Beverly McGuire, Daniel Grigsby, and Cydni Garcia. Also Cassie Jones,

Ellen Jacob, Lynda Castillo, and Howard Klein.

As a well-crafted instrument can bring the subtleties of a musician's creativity to life, I am grateful for friends and clients who allowed me to photograph their homes: Mary and Jack Dant, Leelee and Jeff Durkee, Maggie and Jim Hunt, Ruth Ann and Kevin Huvane, Debbie Jones, Kathryn and Larry Keele, Janet and Mark Lohman, Diana and Harvey Mahler, Lynn Pries, Ginger and Michael Rabkin, Diane and Henley Saltzburg, Cindy and Bill Simon, Maeve and Ted Shugrue, and Susan and Ron Stockdale.

To Bob Asahina, the president of Golden Books, for his vision, conviction, wisdom, and passion.

To Dr. Evelyn Silvers, my kindred soul and teacher.

To Linda Phillips Ashour, one of America's finest novelists, who has blessed me with her unconditional enthusiasm and encouragement.

As a wise man said, "You are who your friends are." If so, I'm very honored to share a lifelong friendship with Dolly Rosen, Kate Hinkle, and Shawn Harris.

To Paul Charles Bailly and Leslie Bailly, my brother and sister, who share my love of architecture and design. And to my mother and father, Virginia and Paul Bailly, who have given me the greatest gift—the gift of their love.

And, most important, to my husband, James Patrick Dunne, who, in a hardened world, is truly a Renaissance man. His artistry, music, sense of story, and intellect enrich not only this book, but also our ever-evolving lives.

Contents

Foreword

When I see my daughter, I see qualities I hope people see in me. I see her passion for design and her career, her joy in raising a family, and her desire to make a difference in the world.

To know Catherine is to know her art. Every time I walk into a home that she has touched, I sense her presence. Her natural sense of balance and beauty creates homes conducive to gracious living. Catherine's theme in this book, "making your home a mirror of your soul," is so true to her work. She exudes the sentiment of this philosophy in every aspect of her life.

Catherine has an extraordinary ability to balance her eclectic academic sophistication with her innocent, passionate, raw joy of design. I can remember her as a young girl as if it were yesterday, fascinated with the elements of design—order, form, texture, and color.

Interior Designing for All Five Senses puts forth a design concept unique and revolutionary in the United States. This book will affect the way interior design will be perceived, approached, and implemented by the professional community and laymen alike.

Rooted in Far Eastern household customs and design practices, this approach is consistent with the growing quest for more-gracious living environments by homeowners. The Japanese teahouse is a good example of an integrated design that embodies all the elements of this concept. The majesty of the teahouse structure visually reveals all aspects of its well-manicured construction.

The senses of taste and smell come alive in the ceremonial making and drinking of the tea. The ritual of kneeling on the floor expresses their oneness with architecture and design, while the thin walls permit one to hear the gentle breezes working their way through the leaves of the bamboo trees. Anyone who has experienced the Japanese teahouse understands how living can be elevated to an art.

A dwelling that is designed for all of the senses allows one to achieve "the art of living." If through design, we encourage and capture this ambience every day, our lives are significantly enriched. Interior design would alter its course in process and perception. The demand for this approach is already out there, and I am very proud that my daughter—through this book—is leading the way.

PAUL BAILLY, AIA, CKD, CCIDC, is Catherine Bailly Dunne's father and one of Los Angeles's most respected architects, with an emphasis in single-family custom residential architecture. He has a master's degree from MIT and he has taught architecture at USC and UCLA. In addition to his practice and teaching, he currently is involved in the archaeological excavation of Maya housing in Belize.

Introduction

I love all the enthusiasm the home is generating these days. The home has become so important that entire shops and exclusive catalogs are devoted to its decorating and upkeep. Decorators (including me) can choose anything and everything to make your surroundings look more beautiful. But, in truth, the best person to decorate your home is you. You are supremely qualified to translate your past and express your personality and desires. I believe anyone can create a beautiful home. All you need is confidence, and the proper tools. This book will give you both.

You'll notice I put confidence first. Mind you, the right tools are important. Precepts, formulas, and technical knowledge are the underpinnings of every successful decorating project, and I'll share those with you. But once that structure is firmly in place, confidence is the secret ingredient that pulls it all together. With confidence, you can transform your home, room by room. Confidence helps you make choices that are right for your lifestyle.

Confidence lets you buy a fabric simply because you love it, not just because it "matches." Confidence allows you to give your home its own unique personality and attitude, instead of marching up banal roads just because they're "safe."

Confidence, in my case, freed me to follow my instincts and desires, and to take a bold new approach to interior design.

I call this approach "Designing for All Five Senses."

DESIGNING FOR ALL FIVE SENSES. Interior design has traditionally focused its energies on pleasing the eye. But a room that looks right doesn't necessarily feel right, and doesn't always seem complete. In an age dominated by the visual, we've come to overlook the rest of the senses—and our world is blander and more irritating for it. Recognizing the power of the senses opens up new pathways of enjoyment.

Appealing to all the senses is the only way to decorate today. When you design for the senses, rooms not only look good, smell good, feel good, sound good, and even taste good, but they have that indefinable "something" that makes you feel at home right away.

You can design a satisfying home when you have tantalized all the senses. In this book, we'll focus on sight, smell, touch, hearing, and taste. As we experience the world, this symphony of senses gathers information that affects us emotionally and physiologically.

Truly, the senses rule.

A House for All the Senses. Everyone wants to live in a comfortable environment where things are easily accessible, a place where you are proud to invite friends. We're attracted to homes that look good and feel right. Life is so complex that home has become the one place where we can relax and soothe body and soul. When you adjust the balance in your home and tune in all the senses, you can enjoy fully the textures of everyday life.

We've all been in rooms that aren't perfect, but feel great. Maybe the windows are small, the floors creak, and the slipcovers are a bit shabby, but when music plays, candles glow around the room, huge tapestry pillows on the sofa invite your touch, and the doors are thrown open to the chorus of crickets, who can help but be entranced?

I want you to take ownership of your house, and take ownership of what you're doing in your house. We need to feed not only our bodies, but also our spirits. Good design finds that amicable balance where all the senses are sparked. When you satisfy the senses, you help satisfy the emotional needs of a healthy family. Without spirit, a bleak air can hover over the most expensive house filled with all the right trappings. A home that speaks to the senses is far more inviting.

When I was a child, our lake house in Minnesota was that kind of place. It wasn't fancy. In fact, it was downright rustic. But everything there seemed more real, more fully alive than our everyday life back in Los Angeles. Those summer memories are still fresh in my mind....

Hot sun on the dock, the feel of warm wood on my back as we sunbathed across the splintery planks. The splish-splash of waves on the sandy shore. The slap of a sunfish as we landed one in the rowboat. White ruffled curtains at my bedroom window. Mosquitoes buzzing by my ear. A screen door slamming, wood against wood, with a hollow clunk. The smell of blueberry muffins, blueberry pancakes, blueberry jam, and the taste of blueberry pie, my fingertips stained soft purple the whole vacation.

After dark, fireflies winking through the tangle of wildflowers by the road. And the shuttered, empty feeling of the rooms as we packed up at the tail end of August. After a month at the lake, I returned home with my senses as finely sharpened as the yellow pencils that I'd bought for school. To me, our summerhouse was a place where all the senses were amply served.

I keep our summerhouse in mind when I decorate today.

RECIPE FOR A HOME. Have you ever stopped "seeing" even the most beautiful room or piece of art because you've lived with it a while? Evoking the senses shakes up the formula a bit, gives things a new spin, and allows you to see from a new perspective. When you decorate for the senses, you "rearrange the furniture" in more than a literal way. It happens step by step, layer by layer. Every time you stimulate another sense, you add another layer to the "cake."

Satisfy the eye first. After all, a room that looks good and works well is the best foundation for an ordered, stress-free life. I'll show you how to set up a plan for your house and choose furniture so that the basics are in place. But don't stop there, as so many people do.

Think about touch. Choose fabrics, surfaces, and textures that make your room come alive.

Then stop, look, and listen. Whether you're buying a piano, carpeting your stairs, installing a new doorbell, or buying a canary—the decisions you make about sound will literally echo through your surroundings.

Decorating for taste is a bit more ephemeral. You'll discover how you can give your home its distinctive taste with creative accessories and collections.

Finally, stir in scents that invigorate, recharge, and refresh, and go far beyond the usual bowl of potpourri (though that's great, too!).

A BOOK

FOR EVERYONE. This is a book for everyone, whether you live in a mansion or a one-room apartment, whether your house is new or one hundred years old, whether you're just starting out or have lived in your place forever. No matter where you live or how you live, it's easy to add new dimensions of comfort and pleasure to the place that you call home.

If you are designing a new house, now is your chance to add a whirlpool tub to soothe your skin, a greenhouse window where you can grow fragrant herbs, and a backyard gazebo to please the eye. If you already have a house and it needs a lift, I'll show you how to "bring the outdoors in," how to put some crowning touches in your home . . . and weave a golden thread throughout your house! When you're decorating for all the senses, you can do two rooms, four rooms, or sixteen rooms—the formula works for all sizes, all scales, all price ranges. And the rewards are enormous.

In short, never underestimate the importance of your home. It fuels your dreams, gratifies your soul, and energizes you each day. Design every aspect of your life to reflect who you are and who you want to be.

My invitation to you? Take my hand, and boldly walk with me through a very exciting new door. Once you enter, you will forever change the way you see, smell, touch, hear, and taste the most beautiful, unique, and spiritual of places—a place that truly is a mirror of your soul . . . .

Your home.

As You Begin

One misconception about creative people is they're messy and disorganized. In truth, it's just the opposite. To be creative, you have to be organized. As a designer, that means doing your homework—taking measurements, doing a budget—whether you're decorating a house, a room, or simply deciding which pillows to use on your sofa.

Then you can enjoy the creative part of designing—appreciating a beautiful fabric, sinking into a chaise—without wondering, "Will it fit?" or "Can I afford this?" When you've done your homework, those questions are already answered.

Separating "homework" from the creative aspects of design allows you to enjoy the artist part of the process. Good designing involves using the tools from both sides of your brain. Doing your homework allows you to be fully creative when you need to be—without distractions.

Have a Plan

Decorating doesn't start with shopping. It starts with a battle plan.

Have a plan for your entire house, even if you're only doing two or three rooms. I can't stress this enough. Too often, people jump into decorating without a plan, and then wonder why the results aren't pleasing.

Always design a thing by considering it in its next larger context—a chair in a room, a room in a house, a house in an environment—an environment in a city plan.
—ELIEL SAARINEN, ARCHITECT AND DESIGNER OF CRANBROOK ACADEMY

A plan gives your house continuity. You don't have to buy everything right away. In fact, I usually recommend doing your house in phases; it's not as overwhelming, and you can pay for it little by little. Two years ago, one of my clients did her living room, kitchen, and dining room, and now we're doing her office, the master bedroom, and the guest room—completing the house.

Even if you can't do the entire house all at once, a plan provides a road map for the future.

If a client tells me, "I want to decorate my whole house, and I have this much money to spend," I say, "Let's get a plan together for the whole house, and then prioritize and see what you can afford now." You may be able to spend a certain amount this year, and in two years, you may have more money to continue the process.

Nailing down a plan for the whole house right in the beginning gives you freedom. You'll know what works into your plan, what to look for on trips—and you can start collecting. Having a plan allows you to take ownership in your house because you know where the house is going.

DO A PRESENTATION. After I meet a client, shop with them, and get to know their tastes, I present my ideas for the decorating I intend to do. This is called doing a presentation. A presentation is the backbone of your decorating plan.

Before you start to decorate, prepare a "presentation" for your house, just as a decorator would do for you. Try running through it with a friend or your spouse. A presentation is

Whistling a happy tune when you feel afraid works just as well in decorating as it does in song. Bold moves and powerful strokes create confidence and clear, energetic results. Decorating with a sure hand begins in the foyer, where a strong first impression makes people feel welcome. This entry has all the right elements: sunny striated walls, a dresser for mail and keys, a mirror to check appearance, plenty of light (a window and a lamp), and a fresh bouquet of roses to extend a fragrant hello. The goblet and plate were specially chosen to point up the curtain's trim.

essential, even if it's for your own use. It consists of three things: your furniture notebook (the "hard" presentation), your fabrics (the "soft" presentation), and, probably the most important element, your floor plan.

The presentation notebook holds your focus. It keeps you organized and sane. When you feel as if you've got this whole house to decorate and it's an overwhelming abyss, you look at your presentation, see what needs to be done next, and carry on. Room by room, you start knocking things off the list, and it looks good, and you feel great about it, and it gets easier and easier.

A presentation notebook saves time. When you're ready to move to the next phase of your project, the presentation notebook includes all your wallpaper and fabrics, already chosen. Decisions have been made. Everything's mapped out. This is a great relief, and allows you to continue with enthusiasm. Without the burden of decisions to slow you down, your project can continue on track.

Don't skip the presentation. There's great satisfaction in creating one and watching it grow, and enormous relaxation when it's ready. It's reassuring to see your presentation notebook sitting on your bookshelf, full of information about what you intend to do in your house—now and in the future.

Consider the whole house before you begin decorating, even if you're going to be tackling just one room at a time. A thoughtfully conceived overall plan gives your house continuity and a sense of peace. I advise my clients to choose their "colors," just as they would for a wedding or a party. My house has lots of green and sienna; maybe you like blue or beige. Taking the long view gives your house cohesiveness. Organize your thoughts by drawing an accurate floor plan, gathering wallpaper samples and fabrics, and organizing everything in a presentation notebook that contains all your dreams.

MAKE A FURNITURE NOTEBOOK. The first thing you need for your presentation is a furniture notebook. I use a big three-ring binder, the kind with pockets inside the cover. Use dividers to organize the notebook room by room, starting with the entry. Create a separate page for each piece of furniture you already own, a page for each thing you intend to buy, and a page for anything structural that needs to be considered, such as a mantel or a stairway that needs redoing. A dictionary would define furniture as movable contents in a room. I expand this definition to include any structural objects that help define the style of a room.

For example, in the "entry" section, you'll probably have a page labeled "Entry Mirror," and another that says "Entry Table," "Entry Lamp," and so on. In the living room section will be pages titled "Living Room Sofa," "Living Room Chair," "Living Room Mirror," "Living Room Mantel," and so forth. Continue this way through each room of the house until you've mapped out everything you want and need. I know this seems like a lot of things to catalog and measure. But once your notebook is complete, you'll have a clear sense of what needs to be done. Then you can proceed at a comfortable pace.

THE PINK PAGES. In my presentation notebooks, I always include a pink page—one for each room—listing things that will stimulate the sense of sight, touch, hearing, taste, and smell. Don't go overboard with this, but if you have a choice between an ordinary bar of soap and one that looks like a petit four, why not go with the petit four? If someone's selling fragrant firewood, stock up. Your dining room chairs will look and feel very different if the seats are made of polished wood or if they are upholstered in suede. It's up to you! Once you begin to design for the senses, new possibilities appear everywhere.

On the pink pages for one of my clients, I see a peach mohair throw for the bedroom, dining chairs with wonderful spiral backs, a backyard smoker, a favorite CD, a cord of piñon wood for the fireplace, and a fish pond to add to her patio. These delights give a house new dimension, and make decorating so much more than just picking out tables and chairs.

CHOOSE YOUR FABRICS. The second part of your presentation is your fabrics, the "soft presentation." There's no notebook for these— just put a piece of tape on the back of each fabric and label it "Living Room Sofa," "Bedroom Chair," or whatever. When you're shopping, it's easy to drop a sample in your purse and run with it. After you accumulate a lot of samples, organize them in manila envelopes, room by room.

A FLOOR PLAN IS YOUR MOST IMPORTANT TOOL. A floor plan is truly your decorating bible. You'll refer to it again and again. Make a floor plan of your entire house, using graph paper and a twelve-foot metal tape measure. (There is also computer software on the market specially designed for this purpose.)

It's much easier to rearrange furniture on a floor plan than to design in an actual room. Take your floor plan on shopping trips so you'll always know if a piece is going to fit.

I like the magnetic planning book *Home Quick Planner* from Design Works, which folds up to the size of a magazine. It includes a big piece of quarter-inch-scale graph paper and an assortment of reusable peel-and-stick furniture, including kitchen appliances and bathroom fixtures. All for less than $20.

No matter how you create a floor plan, be sure to have one. It will help you avoid problems, like having to hoist a sofa through a window by crane because no one realized the sofa was too long to turn a corner near the front door. (They should have had a floor plan!)

Find Your Golden Thread

Every room, every house, needs a theme—something to string the rooms together and make a statement. Themes are so individual. Sometimes it's a color. Sometimes it's a motif. There are three good ways to find your theme and get your creative wheels spinning.

CLIP MAGAZINES. Start by clipping magazines. I ask all my clients to do this. It's a mindless creative exercise. You simply speed through magazines, pulling out what you like. Don't think about the process—just tear and highlight. Use a marker to highlight everything you're drawn to, even if you don't know why you love it. Maybe it's a view of the ocean, or red tulips on the table. Highlight anything that makes you think "I love that."

Highlighting is most important. It helps you remember why you pulled something in the first place. I can't tell you how many times I've set something aside to be filed, and I'll look at it later and think, "Now what was so interesting about that? What did I see here that was so great that I tore up my magazine?" You need to highlight (some people draw arrows or circles) because sometimes you don't see it the second time around.

When you highlight, your theme starts to emerge. There will be a golden thread that runs through all your choices.

Lots of times your theme is something unexpected. Maybe you thought that blue and white was just great because you kept seeing it in all the stores, or you wanted lots of color in your house. But after going through magazines, you find that you really love the neutral palette. The linens, whites, beiges, and creams keep coming up again and again. And you say, "Wow, I really do like those neutral colors; everything I love is a neutral." That's your golden thread.

INTERVIEW YOURSELF. Now, sit down with a fascinating subject—you! With paper in hand, write about the kind of house that you want to have. Growing up, what houses did you

always love and feel comfortable in? What images do you remember? What smells are associated with those houses, those rooms? What colors do you wear? When you flip through a decorating magazine, which rooms do you gravitate toward? What are your favorite things to touch, collect, enjoy—pretty paper and pens, papier mâché boxes, smooth stones, cooking equipment? What sights, sounds, and scents are you drawn to— mountain views, lilacs, crickets chirping, blue hydrangea bushes? Open your mental memory book and let the words flow. You'll probably be surprised at what comes out. Our remembrances are so revealing. For many of us, the rooms of our past still have strong resonance today. Extract from things you

A collection doesn't have to be pure to be pleasing. Reproductions can fill in a collection while you hunt for more of the real thing, or serve as worthy members in their own right. It's hard to tell the originals from the pretenders in this crew of Staffordshire dogs—and, honestly, that's half the fun. Notice how the burled-wood dresser contrasts with the animals, its white top spotlighting the collection.

liked when you were young, or places you've traveled to, read about, dreamed of. Incorporate favorite memories into the house you live in now.

SCOUT THE SHOPS. The most enjoyable parts of my job include shopping with clients, seeing what's new and exciting, and chatting with

Keeping favorite items near at hand is a visual reminder to use each piece more often. This collection got its start when the lettuce vase, fish plates, and tiny vegetable teapots were gathered in a tortoise-bamboo bookcase in the kitchen. The striped green wallpaper is a perfect background, enhancing the green in the pottery.

shopkeepers about what's on the horizon. Part of being a good decorator is knowing the pulse of the market. As you zero in on your theme, take a day or two to do the same thing. Visit your favorite stores, and walk through some new ones, too—not to buy, just to look. Do not limit yourself to home departments and model rooms. Sniff perfumes, listen to new CDs, prowl museum shops and gourmet stores. Notice what strikes a chord as you browse, and take a friend along if you like. Friends can often help discern a pattern in your preferences and interpret your theme, just as a decorator would. All these exercises help crystallize your theme and perk up the senses.

Once, when I was shopping with one of my clients, I noticed that many of the items she was showing me included the color chartreuse. It dawned on me that she was also wearing a T-shirt in that color. Because this client has traditional tastes, I never would have picked chartreuse as her theme. I thought it was too daring for her. But after she pointed out a chartreuse sofa, I realized it wasn't the sofa she liked—it was its color. She wasn't conscious of it at the time, but she kept gravitating toward that color. Chartreuse gave her something exciting—something she didn't have before, something she could call her own—her golden thread.

Everything another client pointed to had birds on it. She had never owned a bird, never thought about birds, but something about birds in flight excited her. We joyously discovered that "birds in flight" was the running theme—her golden thread.

After you've identified your theme, decide how strongly you're going to express it. For some people, it's too much of a statement to express their theme in a fabric. It's a little too permanent. In that case, show your theme in your accessories, as my chartreuse client did. This way, she can put some of it away if she needs to, and bring it out when she feels daring.

For the client with a love of birds, we did a beautiful Chinese wallpaper in her dining room and in her entry—hand-painted with birds in flight. She tells me these are her favorite rooms, rooms in which she can just relax and breathe. For whatever reason, birds in flight make her feel good.

So, find out where your comfort level is. Don't overdo your theme. But don't underplay it, either.

TRY IT ON FOR SIZE. Once you've clipped magazines, interviewed yourself, and scouted the shops, try a theme on for size. This gives you a base to work from. Live with it awhile. Don't be impulsive about your theme, but don't agonize either. No matter what theme you pick, it's sure to be something you love, because it has shown up in your magazine clippings, your memory bank, and the shops you've visited. Once you've discovered your golden thread, base your choices on it and focus your plans.

Make a Budget

One of the truths about decorating is that everything costs more than you think. It's no use having a budget if your prices aren't realistic. Before you make a budget, go back to the stores and write down what things really cost. Magazines and advertisements aren't always a realistic gauge.

Armed with information about the true cost of things, you can prepare a budget for each room without making mistakes. Then decide which rooms are a priority. With a realistic budget, you can comparison shop to find the best combination of quality and price.

INTERPRETING A LOOK. If you can afford something you love, buy it. Otherwise, interpret the look. You don't necessarily have to get a Ming dynasty pot with birds flying on it if you can find something else that will give you that feeling. Often you can extrapolate from very expensive things you see in the stores and get the same look for less. Of course, if you can afford it, then buy the Ming!

BUILDING A COLLECTION. When you are starting a collection, such as Staffordshire, Japanese porcelain, or majolica, you can often blend in reproductions with originals. But it's important to have enough originals in the mix to give the rest of your collection authenticity and credibility.

START SMALL. If you are new to decorating, feel uncertain about making costly decisions, or are nervous about arranging things in your house, my advice is to start small. If you start small, you will always have luck.

Small items are so adaptable. If you buy a miniature chair or ottoman for the living room and it doesn't work there—it's too close to the coffee table, or you can't put your feet up—you can always use it in the bedroom. Put books on it next to your bed, or move it into the family room. There's always a "somewhere" for something small.

The beauty of small things is  that they are usually less expensive, and don't leave you feeling overwhelmed—or nervous. You can take chances with small things, sparking up the living room with a cheetah-print footstool (which is much easier to live with than a cheetah-print chair). And if you get sick of the cheetah print in a year, you can reupholster a small piece inexpensively. Small pieces can also be repainted in a matter of hours, right in your own backyard.

People often are apprehensive buying large, expensive things, such as a chest of drawers. They're nervous they may not like it once they get it home. You'll be more confident about larger purchases as you successfully buy small things, place them in a room, and feel comfortable about your choices. The internal dialogue goes something like this: "Wow, I really love that—it worked out okay. Now [gulp] I'm ready to buy the dining room table."

MAKE ROOM FOR SURPRISES. Leave room in your plans for unexpected finds. Part of the fun of decorating is unearthing gems at antique stores, auctions, flea markets, and estate sales. With your furniture notebook in hand, you'll always know what size you're looking for! This is a great help, because most impromptu finds have to be bought right then and there. When you're prepared, you can take advantage of surprise discoveries.

ANTIQUES ARE NOT INVESTMENTS. As much as I love antiques, they're not really investments. Buy an antique because you love it, because you feel passionate about it right now, not because of its supposed resale value. With antiques, you rarely get your money back. If you do, you may have to wait a very long time.

TAKE YOUR TIME. Building a house over time is so important. When you compromise from the beginning, you'll have to spend more money later to do it over again. It may be redesigning your kitchen, buying new carpeting, or repurchasing a sofa that just never worked.

A lighting designer once told me, "Folks never have enough money to do it right, but they always have enough money to do it over." How true in life—and in design.

Get what you want. You only live once.

THE IMPORTANCE OF SOFAS. A sofa is your most important purchase. It's usually the biggest thing in the room, and often everything else revolves around it.

Take your time with this. Buy a good sofa. This isn't an item to skimp on. A good alderwood sofa frame, as an example, will last twenty or thirty years. The fabric may not last that long, but it's a lot less expensive to recover a sofa than to buy a new one.

The bottom line is that inexpensive sofas don't last. The stuffing starts to shift and the trim comes loose. All the little details that cost money haven't been done, because the manufacturer had to cut corners somewhere.

YOU CAN TAKE

IT WITH YOU. Once you've picked out fabulous things, don't leave them behind if you move. I know a woman who took her kitchen cabinet hardware when she moved, leaving the original hardware she'd replaced and saved. In Europe, everyone takes their curtains when they move; that's not so common here. The curtains in our family room are made of my favorite fabric, a beautiful Lee Jofa hollyhock print. If we ever move, the curtains come with us.

If you know you're going to move, factor it into your decorating plans. Simple window treatments look good anywhere. Buy freestanding pieces, not built-ins. Rather than a tiled backsplash, set pretty tiles or trays upright against the wall.

BE ON THE LOOK. I love being on the look — keeping an eye out for something I plan to buy in the future. Being on the look shows you what the going rates are and allows you to identify a good deal when you find one. Looking at a fine piece, you can see what constitutes quality, and decide which features you care about and which ones you can do without. Sometimes you will be able to find a piece with all the qualities you're looking for at a lesser price. Other times, you buy the most expensive.

LONGEVITY. I believe in longevity. Buy less, and buy better quality. Some people don't understand this. They say, "Oh, I only want it to look good for five years. I'll probably end up changing it, anyway." Those words are like a dagger in my heart. I would rather have you work with a budget, buy less with that budget, and buy great quality that you love.

Why not put your money into a fine piece with long-lasting value instead of purchasing "disposable" furniture? Quality pieces can be passed on from generation to generation, like the twin settees I bought from a friend, and plan to pass on to my daughters. Wait and buy quality when you have the money, instead of buying mediocre things just to get something in the house. If you settle, you'll never love what you have.

Remember, good things look good anywhere. Cheap things look cheap everywhere.

The Six Golden Rules

The process of "decorating" involves many different talents. You need imagination, the ability to dream up a "look." There's mathematics, too: measuring furniture, and making a floor plan. Then there are those endless questions: Where should I start? What fabrics? What colors? How much money and time is this going to take? In short, what exactly needs to be done to make this place look better?

To get going, I always use my Six Golden Rules. These rules will give you direction and launch the job. Use them, and I guarantee your house will take on that extra something that gives it spark and sparkle. These principles will permeate the pages of the book.

1. DESIGN FOR ALL FIVE SENSES.

2. CREATE A FOCAL POINT IN EVERY ROOM.

3. MAKE YOUR HOME A MIRROR OF YOUR SOUL.

4. RESPECT THE STYLE OF YOUR HOME.

5. SUBTRACTING IS OFTEN ADDING.

6. THERE IS NO SUCH THING AS A SMALL ROOM.

1 DESIGN FOR ALL FIVE SENSES. My first golden rule is no surprise. . . . Think of all five senses when you decorate. An interesting room has many facets. A room should be attractive, yes, but like a pretty woman, it should also have something to say for itself. It should smell good, feel good, and taste good, and there should be a hint of life in the air—be it swing music or a canary's insistent trill.

To pull all five senses into your decorating, give each sense equal consideration. Granted, your dining room and kitchen may be strong on taste, your bedroom may emphasize touch, and your porch may be pretty as a picture, but each room should tease all the senses. Answer these questions to see if each room in your home satisfies the senses:

To please the eye, is there color, illumination, a particular focal point?

To tantalize your touch, do intriguing fabrics and textures beckon? Are there surfaces to reach for and stroke?

Besides actual food, are there tempting colors and nourishing sources of light in the room that make you feel satiated and satisfied?

Pleasing the sense of scent is as simple as sniffing the air. How does your house smell? If it comes up short, open the windows, cut some flowers, light a candle, clean the bathroom, crush some spices —bake something!

To satisfy your ears, does every room have a source of music? Are there soft and varied surfaces like carpets, curtains, and bookshelves to absorb unnecessary noise?

Of course, there's that sixth sense—intuition. Sometimes you put something in a room and you don't know why—it just feels right. Or you're shopping and something catches your eye, and you just have to have it. Give in to those impulses. When all is said and done, that particular item may be just the thing that people exclaim over, just the thing that lights you up whenever you walk into the room.

2 CREATE A FOCAL POINT IN EVERY ROOM.
The world's greatest pieces of art share a common attribute: a focal point that draws your eye.

Renoir was a master at creating a focal point. With an imaginative, vivid color contrasting the dominant hue on the canvas, Renoir pulls us into the world of his story. Breathtaking examples include the cherry-colored hat in *Two Sisters on a Terrace*, and the startling red corsage (contrasting with a jet-black dress) in *Riding in the Bois de Boulogne*. My favorite is the majestic blue eyes in *Madame Clapisson*.

The same rules apply when designing a room. A focal point can be created anywhere. Ask yourself where, what, and what color do you want the focal point to be? (Hint: It may not be the dominant color in the room; in fact, it usually isn't.) What texture best captures the personality and soul of the room? Where in the room would you like your guests' eyes to be drawn? To the fireplace? To the sofa? To windows with a fabulous view?

Once you've answered these questions, I promise that ideas will come. Your focal point may be a tangerine pillow on your sofa that brings out the same dynamic color that weaves its way through your draperies, and shows up in the marble hearth of your fireplace. You may find your focal point in a crystal vase of cranberry roses on the mantel, the color and texture of the tender flowers contrasting with the sesame-colored leather on your living room sofa. The focal point of a guest bathroom might be the baby-blue sky of a watercolor picture, contrasting with apricot-glazed walls.

What is the value of having a focal point? Like a handshake, it creates a lasting first impression. Ironically, it is important to arrange furniture so this focal point is discovered rather than emphasized. This is the difference between a refreshing room and a predictable one.

Remember, design is an ever-changing art. Focal points can change, and should! That's the fun (and challenge) of design. One day, your focal point may be those cranberry roses, and the next day, it may be a row of lemon-colored candles lined up on your mantel. You decide where to hang your "Renoir's hat."

3 MAKE YOUR HOME A
MIRROR OF YOUR SOUL. Remember when Goldilocks walked into the Three Bears' house

and tried out their porridge, their chairs, and their beds? Before the bears returned, she had a pretty good idea of who lived there. Take a look around your house. If someone walked in and you weren't home, what would they find out about you?

A home should mirror you and your interests. Your personality may not reveal everything about you, but your surroundings certainly do. I've often been surprised by a client who flags something in a magazine that I never would have picked out for them. Sometimes what you really want can't be expressed in words, but can be shown in your decorating.

Of course, anyone who lives with someone else has to engage in a constant dance of compromise. For years, I've been wanting to frame some drawings I have of urns. I appreciate them for their architectural value, but my husband has no interest in them. Luckily, I have an office, so that's where they'll go. Any woman with a room of her own may have to bring some of these things to her own space.

In the same vein, "Thou shalt not covet thy neighbor's taste." Be daring. Be original. And trust your instincts. Make your house yours, not someone else's.

Sometimes before I decorate a room, I attach an adjective to the space—a word that also describes the person who lives there. We're a friendly family, so I had the word "friendly" in mind when I started to decorate our family room, and that's exactly the kind of room it turned out to be. A client of mine has a library I can only describe as serious, and he's

that way, too—so it works. If you find yourself choosing and discarding ideas one after the other at the start of a project, the adjective game may help you move ahead.

Somewhere in your house, create a "family crest"—a place where you can show and display what's important to you and yours. Whether you live alone or with others, there should be a particular place that celebrates your collective beauty, strength, and glory.

Families like to gather around a fireplace, and visitors are often drawn there, which makes the mantel an ideal place to display your family crest. Your hall might be lined with family photographs. A mudroom can be stenciled with flying fish to show off your family's passion for fishing. Frame your children's drawings and hang them in the breakfast nook.

4 RESPECT THE STYLE OF YOUR HOME. An odd sight caught my eye as I looked out the window on a train trip across the country several winters ago. A totally New England Cape Cod–style house rose up in the middle of the barren midwestern flatlands. The house was out of place in its setting—yet strangely arresting, too. It was obvious that the owners were determined to build their dream house no matter how it fit into its surroundings.

While I admire that kind of chutzpah, I prefer a house that's settled in its place and matches its environment. If you're building, your architect or contractor will help you nestle your project into the site and choose suitable building materials.

Similarly, respect the style of your existing house. A Georgian house doesn't have to be filled with Georgian furniture, but your decorating should probably be more traditional than contemporary. Outside, extend your attention to paint colors, choosing shades that harmonize with the natural surroundings, be they sand and sun, distant mountains, or backyard woods. Landscape with grass, plants, and shrubbery that are native to your area.

5 **SUBTRACTING IS OFTEN ADDING.** Do you know that delicious feeling you get after you throw things out? When clutter is absent, your house can shine. I throw out and give away more than anyone I know. I'd rather live with less and have things I really love than buy things just to fill up a room. Give your "extras" to charity. You'll relish your newfound space.

What about that odd-duck piece that isn't quite right for your house, but you want to keep anyway, such as Great-grandmother's rocking chair that's been in the family for years, or the ornate chest your father carved himself? There are two possible solutions: Point to it or hide it. Because this piece is so different from everything else in your house, you can't treat it like just another piece of furniture. That won't work.

If the piece is important to you, and you really love it, put it center stage in the entry, or somewhere where it can make you smile every time you look at it. Remember, this only works with single pieces. More than one odd duck quickly becomes a flock of strange furniture.

6 **THERE IS NO SUCH THING AS A SMALL ROOM.** Just as they say, "There are no small parts, only small actors," there is no such thing as a small room. Every part of your home is a reflection of you.

Decorating a small room is often the most fun. You can have a good time with it, and it doesn't take a lot of time, money, or wallpaper! I think a powder room tells the most about someone; at its best, it's like a little jewelry box. Foyers are the place to extend a warm welcome—with flowers, with color, with an uncluttered air.

Closets are the ultimate "small rooms." Take a look at yours. Are they black holes filled with who knows what? Instead of closets filled with clutter, why not make them organized and pretty? Browse the stores for the latest gear to help you clean up, clear out, and organize what you have. Line closet shelves with baskets, wire bins, or banker's boxes covered with pretty wrapping paper to hold out-of-season hats, mittens, and scarves.

In your own closet, take a personal view. Paper the walls in a favorite print. Put flowers in your closet; you're in there at least twice a day, maybe more. Use scented shoe stuffers.

Finally, spruce up those oft-forgotten spaces such as porches, basements, and garages. Even mundane replacements like new garbage cans or fresh chaise cushions can go a long way toward improving the quality of everyday life.

So, there you have it—my Six Golden Rules. Remember these secrets and you're on your way to carefree, sensational decorating.

color

light

focus

Spring is tender green young corn and pink apple blossoms....
—VINCENT VAN GOGH, IN A LETTER TO HIS BROTHER, THEO

Designing for the Sense of
SIGHT

Of all the senses, sight has always been the most

emphasized. We live in a visual society, and many of

society's values—prosperity, sophistication, power—can be

represented by physical objects in the home. The challenge

is to have your home represent your values, your beliefs—

your creative soul. Three elements are the backbone of

designing for the sense of sight. If you keep these in your

mind, you'll be way ahead of the game.

They are color, light, and focus. Your challenge: to

creatively blend the colors of a room, to set a mood with

lighting, and to focus a room's personality and attitude

through various objects in the room.

Color

Color is the fastest way to spark the sense of sight. Color reaches beyond the limits of construction and architecture, extending walls, raising or lowering ceilings, and eliminating corners with its magical powers.

Imagine, for a moment, an exquisite meal, but eliminate all the seasonings, sweeteners, and spices. A soup without its salt. Lemonade without its sugar. Color is nature's sweetener, giving design its flavor, its excitement, its personality. But as with a wonderful meal, proportion is everything. Too much of any seasoning can spoil the soup.

Our bodies and emotions respond to color

Tomato red is said to make people salivate, so it's an obvious color choice for any room where food is served. The owners of this home chose red walls for their dining room. Not only does red stimulate the taste buds, but it also looks great with the Flemish painting. The bouquet of flowers set in front of the painting adds another dimension, and looks as though it erupts from the scene. The sideboard includes an array of gleaming silver, figurine lamps, and black candles as dramatic as wands. The table's brimming urn of fruit is a delicious centerpiece.

in such predictable ways. Restaurant designers know they can excite us simply by painting the walls red. In a bedroom, red may rob you of sleep, while in a dining room, tomato-soup walls are delicious. The inside of a linen closet painted raspberry red, or a red front-hall closet, can be pleasantly provoking. Red stimulates, attracts energy, and makes everyone hungry; our metabolism increases almost 14 percent when we see red. Red apples on a table or red roses in a vase attract the eye, as the sense of touch, smell, and taste come into play, too. We are drawn to red like a magnet. Use red judiciously; it tends to dominate a color scheme.

Of all the colors, green is my favorite. Green is so natural. It brings the outdoors in and effortlessly goes with everything. Green is

SIGHT AND THE BRAIN

Most of what we know is gathered from the sense of sight. This sense is so important that a quarter of the brain's cortex is devoted to processing sight signals. Highly visualized nerve cells called neurons respond to different stimuli such as color, form, or motion. The brain stores information by linking neurons into pathways. These pathways are unique to each person, built through our individual experiences with the world. Messages sent along the nerves are received by all parts of the body. When the sense of sight is damaged, the other senses take over to translate the world.

calming. Muted greens are soothing to the eye, while vibrant greens add life to a room. Green promotes balance and careful judgment. Paint your library green, and plant leaf-green cushions on green wicker furniture. I love the look of green with my favorite flower, roses—and any combination of pink and green. My house is done in muted greens and siennas.

Yellow is warm. It gives you the feeling that sunlight is streaming in from outside. Butter-yellow walls are always wonderful. Citrus yellow makes a strong statement—be sure your other colors are equally strong or they will fade away. Yellow is great in an entry because of its cheerful qualities. Yellow and blue is a winning combination that's particularly nice in kitchens. Yellow is also the color of dance. Hang banana-yellow curtains in your exercise room.

Blue is a nature color—calm and relaxing. The refreshing crystal blue of the ocean and the bright clear blue of the sky bathe you in serenity. For heavenly dreams, paint your bedroom a beautiful pale blue. As with many colors, blue is a chameleon—dark blue is strong and proud, while light blue is soft and kind.

If your room has an unusual quirk, make the most of it. This little bay makes a delightful place to sit. Tall windows festooned with red-and-white curtains frame a pleasant outdoor view and staggered plates direct the eye skyward, where a whimsical balloon chandelier takes flight. Green glazed walls give the whole space its calming, soothing atmosphere.

Black is dramatic—a wonderful accent. Small enameled tables, picture frames, curtain rods, and floor lamps look sculptural in black, jumping out in relief, especially when silhouetted against a light background.

White can signal escape. Snowy lace bed curtains can seem ethereal. White gives the image of clean, wide-open space. Nothing is better for reflecting and amplifying light. White is daring because everyone wonders how you'll keep it clean! It's a symbol of purity, freshness, and confidence.

Many designs favor the neutral palette because it is classic and never goes out of style. A mix of oyster, eggshell, ivory, ecru, and snow is timeless. For a look that's totally new, blend many subtle neutrals in one room, letting one color drift into another. Enhance the neutral palette with lots of texture: a wood or limestone floor, nubby upholstery. Then give the room tempo by adding spots of color here and there: pillows, candles, flowers, picture frames, and linens. For a new look that can be done inexpensively, change these accent pieces from time to time. By changing the color of your accessories, you'll give a room an entirely different personality.

When you choose a color, don't think

TO INCREASE THE PLEASURES OF A LARGE ROOM

Let one pale color predominate to unify the space and rest the eyes.

Lift the ceiling with a light shade. Pale blue ceilings seem to fly.

Pump more-intense color into small objects and areas of the room: a deep green sleeping alcove off a pale green living room. Or a lipstick-pink slipper chair in a light pink room.

Screens, rather than art, will add dimension to empty corners.

too much about it. Let your right brain find a color that just feels good. Some of us find decorating inspiration in nature, drawn by the soothing tones of sugar-sand beaches or soft green hills. For others, nothing less than a joyous mélange of Mardi Gras colors will do. New ways of combining colorful possessions, even clothing, can lead you to discover new decorating paths. You can even dictate the wall color for an entire room with something as small as the tiny accent colors in a piece of fabric.

To test a color, paint large illustration boards and hold them against walls and furniture. Take the sample boards with you when you shop, and you'll always know if you've made a match.

A simple room often makes more of an impact than one that's done to death. The color duet of periwinkle and white gives this airy bathroom all the freshness of a Mediterranean isle. The simple background lets strong architectural elements stand out: the silver-footed tub with sculptural plumbing, the raftered ceiling.

Shouldn't your bathroom be as sophisticated as any other room in your house?

Pastels usually predominate in powder rooms, so this black-and-white bath with painted cabinets and toile wallpaper is all the more striking. To open up the room and reflect its airiness, a large mirror hangs over the sink. Its rich gold frame is decidedly unbathroomlike. Equally sophisticated are the silver-framed photographs clustered on the counter, the skirted chair and dog pillow, the sisal rug, and the fat tassel hanging from the cabinet door.

AQUARIUMS ARE LIVING COLOR. Aquariums offer up an ever-changing picture. I've installed them in offices, kitchens, bathrooms, and even in bedrooms. Aquariums can be hypnotizing by day, and the bubbling water will lull you to sleep at night. A fresh-water tank houses classic goldfish and colorful African cichlids, while a saltwater tank supports tenants with more exotic hues. Children and adults alike may find that staring at an aquarium can be far more fascinating than a television screen.

KOI PONDS ARE

A YEAR-ROUND FASCINATION. Koi are big, colorful cousins to goldfish, and their ponds provide an eyeful of color. Track the hide-and-seek taking place beneath the lily pads of an indoor or outdoor koi pond, and you'll be rewarded by the sight of these easy-to-care-for swimmers that can live for a hundred years.

Build a room of restful pales as a refreshing break from trends and temporary fashions. Start from the ground up with a sisal area rug. Upholstery should be almost colorless, but have texture, touch, and subtle pattern. In this room, the furniture is covered with velvet, a textured cotton, a leafy print, or soft stripes, all in shades of green and beige. The colors emphasize the room's rich wood and tortoise tones. The simplicity of the curtains adds to the size of the room.

Light

Bad lighting is painfully obvious, while good lighting is like a dragonfly—you hardly know it's there. For a room that's most flattering to people and interiors, remove heavy curtains and blinds, unnecessary window shades, and superfluous sheers, and let in oceans of natural light. After dark, light candles and turn on pink lightbulbs in every room to shed a warm glow.

PINPOINT YOUR LIGHTING. Always light objects, not spaces. When you light an object, it generates light back into the room. If you light everything the same way, nothing stands out. Instead, light one thing differently to make it more important. Highlight a bookcase filled with French books you particularly love, or framed photographs of your family on an occasional table, using lamps, pin spotlights on a track, lanterns, candles, or a combination of these. A low-wattage bulb in a pendant lamp can pick out a small table in a quiet corner or focus light on a special painting, sculpture, or your grandmother's baby chair.

WASH THE WALLS WITH LIGHT. If you want soft, gentle illumination in your hallway, bounce light off the walls with a ceiling-mounted wall washer on a track. Lighting vertical surfaces always makes a space seem larger. This works in kitchens and bathrooms, too.

A GREAT LAMPSHADE MAKES THE LAMP. To turn an ordinary lamp into an eye-catching treat, find an unusual lampshade. Search for foil-lined shades, pierced shades, and tasseled shades at lamp shops, antique stores, and consignment shops.

Foil-lined shades make light sparkle, and look pretty when you catch a glimpse inside the shade, glistening like a silvery petticoat or a hammered gold cloak.

Shades with designs pricked out or cut into the surface can pick up floral or graphic themes in your room. When my daughter was a baby, her bedroom lamp had a shade pierced with roses that were watercolored in pink and green.

Lighting a room is as easy as pointing a flashlight when you illuminate objects instead of the space itself. This Biedermeier chair and table are pooled with light from an Indian-motif lamp, while a picture light focuses attention on the painting. Frankly, that's all the light this small space needs, and the effect is far softer than if it were lit from above. The objects, too, are carefully edited for maximum effect. The gold tones of the wooden chair enhance the gold picture frame, the table's gold edging, and even the doorknob.

Tasseled shades look dainty in small sizes, and have an elegant Victorian feeling. Pair them with glass or crystal lamp bases.

LIGHT UP THE NIGHT. Arriving home after dark, it's comforting to see lights on. Take advantage of timers and motion detectors to create a visual welcome. Set your front door light and a lamp in your entry on timers so you'll always be able to find your keys—and will never have to walk into a dark house late at night.

Motion detectors can illuminate the backyard or driveway when your car pulls in, snap on lights in an entire wing of the house as your kids run up the stairs, and light up a hallway to help a sleepy child find the bathroom or her parents' room at night.

COLORED GLASS
CREATES A RAINBOW. If there is a "down" time of day at your house when the light begins to fade, brighten things up with colored glass bottles on the windowsill. One of my clients has blue and green bottles in the arch above her

> In decorating, no detail is unimportant. Think of lamps and lampshades as art or fashion, searching for exciting, out-of-the-ordinary styles. This Chinese urn was made into a lamp and topped with an Oriental finial. Silhouetted by the light, the toile fabric shade with a chinoiserie shape looks as delicate as a paper cutting and brings the outdoor garden inside. The silver plate stand of apples tempts the taste buds.

French doors. The light shining through the bottles echoes the sun's journey across the sky, filling her family room with the shades of grass and sky. The bottles look decorative even when there is no sun; glass in itself is soothing to the eye. In your bookcases, consider glass shelves instead of wooden ones. Hang an old or new stained-glass window in front of a window and light it to show off its intricacies.

LIGHT TUBES. When the pitch of your roof is too deep for a skylight, consider installing a light tube as you're building the house. These round, clear cylindrical tubes go all the way up to the roof, bringing outdoor light into dark corners of your house. I love the way they open up space and brighten hallways. Unless you are very skilled in this department, hire a contractor for these types of jobs. You can order skylights or tubes through your contractor.

LIGHT UP YOUR CLOSETS. When you open a closet to find something, being able to see what's inside is half the battle. I have an automatic light in my clothes closet that goes on when I open the door, triggered by a button in the doorjam. An electrician can easily install the same device in a linen closet, a foyer closet, or the cupboard where you store place mats and tablecloths.

USE LANTERNS TO POINT
THE WAY. When you're having a party, use the subtle winking lights of candle lanterns and candelabra to guide people through the house.

These old-fashioned illuminators have an Old World feeling, shed a pleasant light, and can be moved around the house in dramatic fashion, creating intimacy wherever they are set.

When we have parties, I station candle lanterns here and there: in the entry, in the hall outside the living room, and in the hall leading to the powder room. If I'm serving food in an area that's not the main food area, and I want people to gravitate there, I use lantern light to lead them. Chandeliers and sconces, though not mobile, can create the same effect.

DIM THE LIGHTS. Put all your lights on dimmers. It's easy to do, even in an older house, and it is a surefire way to create a mood.

DIM THE POOL. To give your backyard pool the moody aura of a pond, put your pool lights on a dimmer. Remind your professional electrician that the dimmer must be able to handle the increased wattage of the pool lights.

LIGHT THE OUTDOORS. If you want to turn on your Christmas lights with ease, install a weatherproof outlet under the eaves. A light switch controls the outlet indoors. My neigh-

> ## To Make a Large Room Seem More Intimate
>
> Place a round library table in the center of the room, topped by a huge flower arrangement in an urn.
>
> Paint the walls a dark color.
>
> Line the walls with bookcases the same color as the walls.
>
> Lower the ceiling, add character, and unify the space with crown moldings, chair rails, and picture rails painted white to reflect light.

bor did this, and she can turn on her holiday lights in an instant, while I'm outside, plugging lights into extension cords dangling from my window!

Create festive party lighting by twisting strands of tiny white lights around the top railing of your deck. It looks so pretty at night—your own year-round galaxy of starlight.

SEARCH OUT UNUSUAL LAMPS. Some people try to make their lamps invisible. Don't go that route—treat lamps as if they were jewelry or little pieces of art. Choose unusual lamps and put them in unexpected places to give them more importance.

I saw the most whimsical pair of lamps on vacation last year and I wish I'd bought them. The lamp base was a little monkey holding an umbrella tipped to the side, and the umbrella

For centuries, bits of glass have delighted the eye. Colors sparkle when light shines through stained-glass windows, mosaics, or shaded bottles. Everyone notices the sapphire glow from this line of blue glass vessels and vases set on a high window ledge. The backdrop of lace, simply tacked up with pushpins, softly filters the sun.

hid the lightbulb. When you walk into a room, lamps like these aren't overlooked; they're part of your display.

In a bathroom, dimmers can adjust the intensity of wall sconces and ceiling lights, the kind you usually have to put up with. But for real atmosphere, I love using little lamps in the bathroom. When you get up in the morning, make a ritual of turning on the lamps to enjoy their gentle light.

SET THE STAGE. Take a tip from theatrical designers, and light a room as if it were a stage set. Ask yourself, "What's going on here? Is this a watching-TV scene? A conversation scene? A reading scene? A cuddling scene?" Then buy exactly the kind of lights you'll need to set that mood.

ASK THE EXPERTS. Rely on the professionals when an unusual lighting challenge presents itself. I've seen the most ordinary settings transformed into spectacular displays under the knowing guidance of lighting consultants.

I love to bring the outdoors into master bathrooms. The design of this room changes drastically just by opening one of the bay windows; in one sweep you've invited the senses: the sight of nature's best work, the smell of roses below, the harmony of birds in the morning, and the touch of a wandering breeze.

Focus

*Some people like to make a little garden out
of life—and walk down a path.*

—JEAN ANOUILH, *The Lark* (ADAPTED BY LILLIAN HELLMAN)

THE IMPORTANCE OF MEMENTOS. If you furnish your house with things that don't mean anything to you, no matter how expensive or trendy they are, it will never feel like your house. No matter what decorator you bring in, no matter whom you pay top dollar to, it will not be your home until you bring in personal items that you've picked up over the years.

When you travel, it's so important to buy one item on the trip that you'll have as a memento. I guarantee that every time you look at it, you'll remember the wonderful time you had. I do this with my girls. I allow each of

Collections don't need a pedigree to be fun. This pack of canines ranges from porcelain to cast iron, with only their doggy attributes and low price as linking factors. Once the dogs outgrew their desktop kennel, the collection spilled over to a hanging shelf that coordinates with the rustic desk. Notice how a small bouquet of colorful fresh flowers enlivens the company.

39

them to buy one special thing on vacation, so they can begin to see the importance of their memories—and how they conjure up those treasured feelings. (At this age, my youngest will usually choose a Barbie doll, but there's nothing I can do about that right now!)

Memories are made of these small things, and that's what homes are made of. It's not about going into an antique store, buying a tableful of stuff, bringing it home, and setting it on your table. A house is a treasure chest for personal family mementos. Like my little green clock from England...

THE LITTLE GREEN CLOCK.

When I was first married, my husband and I took a much-needed ski vacation with our newborn daughter. In a shop window, I spotted a little green clock made in England. The clock was a little extravagant, and my husband said, "We don't need a clock." But I knew there were at least three places in our house where we needed a clock, and I was always running into another room to see what time it was. I said, "No, I'm getting it," and I bought the clock. And I'm so glad I did.

That little green clock means so much to me. It's up in the girls' bathroom now, but it has moved all around our house. And every time I

TO MAKE A SMALL ROOM SEEM LARGER

Set a fresh tone with ecru walls and a white ceiling.

Use large tiles or large area rugs on the floor for a "no boundaries" effect.

Use low furniture, or eliminate furniture, using just a few large-scale pieces.

Emphasize the vertical with wall moldings, slim floor lamps, narrow window treatments, and vertical stripes in fabric, wallpaper, or paint.

Avoid window coverings with fussy top treatments.

---

look at that clock, I can practically taste those days when we had our first real vacation as a family. We had a wonderful time; we had little money, and although at the time it was such an extravagance, I will always have that clock. I don't have to dig out the photo album or look at a video to remember that trip because I see the clock every day. As time marches by so quickly, the ever-moving pace of our family stops for just a moment every day when I look at my green clock.

WINDOWS ARE THE EYES OF A ROOM.

Decorator show-houses are often held in older homes with mismatched windows, narrow windows, and windows that are hopelessly out of date. Yet the rooms still manage to look great, in good part because of the window treatments. A window's proportions are a given, but there are ways to make all windows look better.

Your room will have a pulled-together look if all your window treatments match, especially

What makes this so inviting and alive? By framing the fruit and flowers inside the natural glow of garden sunlight, we welcome the energy of life streaming into the room.

in newer homes, where there are so many more windows per house than there used to be. Hang curtains or valances at the same height around the room, equidistant from the ceiling.

A short window will look taller topped with a wooden cornice or with curtains hung above the actual window frame.

Older windows are usually smaller than new ones. Make a narrow window look wider without blocking the view by topping the curtains with a swag made of two-color cording. Swag double rows of cord as if they were fabric, finishing each end with a decorative tassel that drops to each side.

A vertically striped fabric or patterned lace will give the illusion of height to a window that's wide and squat.

Sometimes all you want to do is make an unappealing window "disappear." In this case, paint the woodwork and walls the same color—and choose a simple window covering or blind in the same color. A very large window seems to diminish in size when a wide lace panel is shirred across the glass.

Make the most of your stairwell. It's a home's minigallery, where wide-open soaring space can tantalize the eye. This is the perfect place to enhance the entirety of a collage, a set of prints, photographs, or mirrors. Use a rug's pattern or border like a yellow brick road, to lead the eye where you want it to go. In this home, portraits of beloved four-legged companions line the walls, while the needlepoint runner's flower medallions draw attention upward.

Uncurtained windows are terrific, but sometimes glare is a problem. Freestanding screens can be moved around the room at will to block the windows when necessary, and they fold up when not needed. Or diffuse the light in a delicate way by veiling windows with thin bamboo shades or textured curtains of voile, lace, or striped sheer linen.

In truth, I prefer neutral curtains in most rooms. The backdrop of subtle curtains allows people and objects to shine.

ART INHABITS A ROOM. Art stimulates the eye and brings a space to life. It mirrors your soul and tells people who you are. In any room, art is the ingredient that completes the picture. Without art, it seems as if no one lives in your house.

When buying a piece of art, ask yourself, "Do I respond emotionally?" Buy only things you love. Don't try to match your sofa or balance a piece of art in a neighboring room. A good painting stands on its own merits and works anywhere.

Hang the middle of the piece of art at eye level (no higher). If you have art pieces of various sizes, line up the bottoms, giving a sense of continuity.

It's better to own one beautiful piece of art than three inferior pieces. A high-quality poster from a museum shop, nicely framed, will bring you more pleasure than a purchase made simply for the sake of owning original art.

Remember that art is long-term. Investment should never be your primary consideration.

As with antiques, buy a piece of art because you love it, not because you think you'll make money reselling it someday. The highest-quality painting will always have a market.

THE MAGIC OF MIRRORS. Mirrors are a marvelous way to expand a room's horizons, making the space seem twice its size. The larger the mirror, the larger your room will look.

If you have a window that overlooks a stunning outdoor scene, enjoy the landscape twice by hanging a mirror on the opposite wall. Before you hang a mirror permanently, hold it up to make sure it reflects the best view.

ENGAGE THE EYE. Narrow beaded boards, tongue-and-groove paneling, chair rails, and wainscoting bring out the finest qualities in a room, just as a frame highlights a piece of art. Geometry and symmetry have enormous eye appeal. Pick out the details in any wooden molding by lightly highlighting grooved or sunken areas with a paintbrush dipped in semitransparent silver or gold paint. Before you paint, wipe the brush until it is almost dry. If the lines look slightly crooked, so much the

Consider pictures and prints in the context of your room instead of as separate entities. This way, they are drawn into the decor instead of just being stuck on top. These botanical prints matted in green are, in effect, framed once more by white panels on the marbled walls. Pencil-thin lines of silver and gold shadow the panel moldings. The arrangement's ordered symmetry is a comfort to the eye.

Trompe l'oeil painting is meant to fool the eye. It is often employed to bring a sense of the outdoors inside. In this city kitchen, a favored cow visits his owners "through the kitchen door" as a reminder of their farm in the country. The illusion extends to the pretend panes—the door is actually smooth.

better—the handcrafted quality makes this detailing so charming.

TROMPE L' OEIL. "Trompe l' oeil" is French for "fool the eye." It's one of my favorite design tools, and it can do wonders in giving a room

visual depth, personality, and a sense of humor.

This technique was practiced extensively by the ancient Greek and Roman painters, but it exploded during the Renaissance. Artists would paint pictures on interior and exterior walls of buildings, giving the deceptive impression of a three-dimensional image. It was common to see imaginary windows and doors on plain walls, often with people and animals in the background.

But a little bit goes a long way. We have ivy painted around the frame of our guest bathroom window, and a little bird that appears to be perched on the window frame. It also is a terrific way of bringing outdoor images into your home.

An interior designer friend told me about a client who wanted fat molding around a doorway in her bathroom. They took the easy road. Instead of building it with wood, they just painted a fantasy molding on the wall, adding a pretend bird's nest on top for good measure. Everyone who sees this doorway smiles and exclaims over its charm. Maybe there's a place in your house that deserves some fool-the-eye painting.

Somewhere in your house, treat yourself to small doses of luxe materials and effects, whether it's a painted finish on the walls of a small powder room, or a few yards of fabric for a special chair. Feeling experimental? It's fun to try your ideas on a small piece of furniture. A tiny chair or ottoman can handle fabrics and trim that might be overwhelming in large doses. And expensive remnants are affordable when you need only a few yards of fabric. This ottoman marries two different fabrics for a more formal look: its velvety plaid base topped with a red chintz pillow is edged with fringe and velvet bows.

What is your family's passion? Is it hearts, sailing, travel, cats, Norway? Let your house announce that passion the way this one does. It's plain to see the lifetime love of the sea signaled by this collection of all things nautical: model ships, seashells, beach glass, life preservers, starfish, and two denizens of the deep. Showing off the things that are dear to you allows people a glimpse of your soul.

CATHERINE BAILLY DUNNE
· Interior Design ·

THE LITTLE HOUSE
AN ARCHITECTURAL SEDUCTION
JEAN-FRANÇOIS DE BASTIDE

SPEND EXTRA ON EVERYDAY THINGS. The things we see most often are the things we use every day. Replace tired place mats, candles, and vases at least once a year—and bring in dramatic new replacements. Find an attractive broom and welcome mat, buy fresh dish towels and pot holders, and use a bright new sponge. Occasionally, try a color, brand, or style that wouldn't usually be your choice, just for variety. Little things will brighten your days—far more than an expensive appliance that spends most of its time in the cupboard.

MAKE A SPLASH IN EACH ROOM. Exercise your sense of sight by placing an eye-catching "something" in every room. Transform a bed with a thick throw of wool or fake fur. Dominate the center of the living room with a big, square button-tufted ottoman. Fill a vase with very tall flowers for the bedroom or dining room. Hang an oil painting over your bathtub.

Do you have a favorite collection? Mine is silver. I love to stroke its surface, and watch it gently age with time. My desk is a symphony of silver accessories. Photographs look wonderful in silver frames, whether they're color or black and white. My grandmother's silver creamer is my pencil cup, and a silver toast rack from England holds letters. I'm hooked on silver cigarette holders, and always search for them at antique stores.

GROUP ORDINARY OBJECTS

AS SPECIAL DISPLAYS. Fill a basket with things you're interested in to give a room a "look." For a client whose teenage son loves athletics, I piled a huge old basket full of sports balls of all kinds. It not only organized them, but also showed off the young man's passion.

Maybe you collect exotic bath oils. Imagine these bath oils displayed on a bathroom windowsill or the edge of a tub. Bottles filled with seashells, pearls, citrus curls, or a sprig of eucalyptus engage the eye. Reflect your love of the sea, and invite the sense of touch, too, with a dish of sea glass and sea urchins.

EVERY ROOM NEEDS A PLANT. The sight of trees and flowers literally brings a room to life; any space is unfinished without them. But they don't have to be real. I always seem to pick the wrong plant, put it in the wrong corner, and two months and $45 later, I'm left with nothing.

If you travel a lot, don't want the responsibility of caring for plants, or have a brown thumb like me, try pressed ferns framed under glass. Or maybe pillows screened with flower prints, botanical trays, playing cards, coasters, and dishes, or a huge museum poster of tomatoes, like the one my friend Dolly has in her kitchen.

But whenever possible, there's no substitute for the real thing.

BRING SILVER ACCESSORIES

OUT OF HIDING. Silver reflects light and brings luster, sparkle, and shine to a room.

Old silver becomes so gentled with use that it almost feels soft. Store letters in a sterling toast rack on a desk. Fill a silver bowl in the bathroom with cotton balls. I use old silver cigarette holders as small vases to add sparkle in unexpected places around my house; about three inches tall, they look like little urns.

FIND THE FIRELIGHT. When you feel like a fire in the fireplace but the weather's too warm, light candles in your fireplace—it looks gorgeous. Stagger the candles across the stacked logs, mixing votives and tapers of different sizes, or use all-of-a-kind candles arranged in graphic procession. I think white candles look the prettiest. This is a great idea for climates like mine here in southern California, where the warmth of a fire isn't always needed, but the cheer is always welcome. I call these summer fires.

There are other ways to dress up a hibernating fireplace. In the firebox, the interior section of your fireplace, place a bouquet of birch logs up-ended in a big copper kettle. Or dress up a fireplace with an old-fashioned painted wooden fire screen. Or you may want to put an oversized basket of dried flowers in the fireplace.

To get the most enjoyment from your fireplace, use it year-round. Candles set a summer hearth ablaze, giving the effect of a fire without all the heat. For the most impressive display, light your tallest pillars on the floor, and balance vanilla-scented votives behind them on a stack of logs. Interspersing the logs with lengths of white birch creates a snowy masquerade.

Sometimes a collection takes on a life of its own. This triple-decker display of global dancers is set in a charming whitewashed cottage-style hutch. The collection began as a set of Dutch figurines and grew to encompass the world. Trusting in the whimsy of the arrangement allowed the community to grow. And, like a good party, crowding is good. Remember—there's strength in numbers, and two of anything can be the start of a great collection.

A Few Miscellaneous Thoughts

VISUALIZE WITH BROWN
PAPER TEMPLATES. When a client has a hard time visualizing how a piece will look in a room, I often cut out a brown paper pattern and lay it on the floor. A roll of brown paper

(thirty-six inches wide) is the same depth as most sofas. One of my clients couldn't decide between a forty-eight-inch and a fifty-four-inch round dining room table. She knew the room was a little small for a fifty-four-inch table, but she thought the advantage of seating more people might outweigh the inconvenience of tight quarters. Laying two different brown paper templates on the floor, she quickly saw that the smaller table was best. Some piano companies will send you a floor pattern so you can visualize the impact a piano will have on your room.

FOLLIES. Follies are a way to bring amusement and wit into a room. In France and England, architects always included a visual folly somewhere in the distance outside the great palaces as a place for the eye to focus on and rest. Back then, it may have been a gazebo or garden statue. Today, it could be an amusing needlepoint pillow, a pretend rooster in your foyer with real birdseed scattered at his feet, or a garden scarecrow.

Follies lighten the spirit of a room. They can appeal to any or all of the senses. Throughout the book, you'll find examples of follies that appeal to the senses. You will surely think of other ones that may be particularly appro-

---

TO EMPHASIZE THE PLEASURES OF A SMALL ROOM

Engage the eye with pattern and color.

Use small tiles or mosaics to add charm, intimacy, and quaintness.

Paint the walls a deep, warm shade.

Save space with built-ins.

Bring down a high ceiling with a dark color.

---

priate to your home, your family, and your own unique sense of humor.

Follies are well suited to weekend and vacation homes, where the mood is relaxed and casual. In the kitchen of her lakeside cottage, my friend painted a mousehole (a trompe l'oeil) on the wall by the stove and, near it, a small mouse nibbling a wedge of cheese. This little folly never fails to elicit smiles.

My friend Kate and her husband raise chickens. Before a party, she always places a hard-boiled egg on a black satin pillow and sets it on a table in a quiet corner. This always gets conversation going!

In conclusion, create a home that looks beautiful to you. With imaginative choices of color and lighting, you are on your way to painting a stunning and telling self-portrait. Now you're ready to build upon this strong visual base, involving the other senses, one by one.

incense

flowers

candles

It is not sight or sound that, when a heart forgets, most makes it to remember; it's some old poignant scent re-found—like breath of April violets, or apples in September.

—NANCY BYRD TURNER, *YEARS AFTERWARD*

Designing for the Sense of
SMELL

Nothing is more memorable than a favored scent.

Piquing the sense of smell sets a mood. The ancient

Egyptians knew this when they danced through the warm

nights wearing hair combs filled with perfumed fat.

The fat would melt and drip down, glistening and

scenting their bodies. Medieval ladies never went anywhere

without a silver scent ball attached to their waists; they

surrounded themselves with a spicy aura to hold strong

street smells at bay. Some Middle Eastern mosques are

still held together with aromatic mortar.

Scent
the Air

If you want people to remember your home, give it a distinctive scent.

Studies have proven that a signature scent can make you and your home more memorable, but I don't need a study to tell me that. Whenever I smell carnation soap, I think of my grandmother. I used to shop at a small clothing store that always smelled great, and everything I bought there smelled like that, too. I have a book that smells so good I can't stop burying my nose in its pages; once upon a time, it must have been the home to a scented bookmark. Pleasant smells evoke peace and calm, just as surely as the "wrong" smells set you on edge. It's a powerful impetus to make your home smell its best.

The scent you choose will be as individual as you are. One person leans toward homey cinnamon and sprightly lime; exotic frangipani and sandalwood entrance another. Some like incense; others prefer energizing peppermint. It takes some time to find a scent for your home

Freshen a bowl of potpourri by laying dried flower heads and fruits on top. You can also use drops of fragrant oil to add a stronger scent, if desired. Because potpourri is dried and has a muted tone, it teams well with old books and antiques.

that the whole family can agree on. Once you do, use that scent wherever you can.

Lately, I've been intrigued by candle-powered lamps and ceramic diffusers that vaporize essential oils. The candle and the fragrance promote balance and renewal; enjoy them when you're meditating or doing yoga poses. You'll set different moods depending on which oils you use. Juniper is invigorating; I like clary sage and geranium because they are relaxing.

For fragrance every time you turn on the lights, try a terra cotta or metal ring that balances on a lightbulb. Put a few drops of oil onto the ring. When the bulb heats the oil, its scent will fill the room. For a similar effect, you can dab the cool bulb with a few drops of oil before you turn on the light.

Revive a flagging potpourri by adding a few drops of rose, lavender, or tuberose oil. Toss it like a salad, and top the mixture with small bundles of lavender sprigs—or dried flower heads of zinnias, larkspur, roses, and pressed pansies. Pour the potpourri into an antique china bowl, and fill it to the brim.

Repetition is essential in any successful decorating project. It's the drumbeat that makes a room hang together. The advice seems elementary, but having a recurring theme helps define your space. In this living room, the theme is tulips. The sofa's floral upholstery is underscored by a bouquet of real tulips on the table. The fabric's motif and colors are emphasized by needlepoint pillows. Can you hear the drumbeat?

Fruits,
Flowers, and
Other Plants

NATURE'S PERFUMERY. When I went to the Getty Museum in Los Angeles, I was mesmerized by the big urns filled with lemon verbena. Running your hand over the leaves releases a delightful citrus scent. Bring your hand to your mouth, and your lips pucker. Lemon verbena is a leafy, lacy perennial that grows year-round in temperate climates and thrives best when planted outdoors in the sun. It can be brought indoors to tantalize guests for a short time. I ordered some at my local nursery, and now I have pots of lemon verbena growing in my garden at home. I put a pair of plants on the table in my foyer during parties, and another in the powder room. Really, any

When this little Kaffir lime tree gets bigger, it will spread its sweet scent through the house. In warm weather, it can live outside on the deck. For now, the tree is planted indoors near a hand-tinted photograph of a sweet young lady, another fast-growing sprout. A dish of fresh limes was placed beside the tree, their skins pricked with a toothpick to add a tangy freshness to the air.

60

live shrub in a pot will add a bold piece of greenery to your interior landscape. If it smells good, all the better.

The Kaffir lime tree is another plant that produces abundant scented and aromatic leaves, and thrives inside and outside in gentle climates. The leaves can be used in salads, and the plant will produce tasty limes.

Some flowers are so sweet they can fill your whole house with a heady perfume. I always look for these at the florist—gardenias, stargazer lilies, freesia, and roses. The roses smell even stronger once they've bloomed. With their reputation for romance, you might think red roses smell the best, but they're usually not as fragrant as roses of other colors.

In the garden, you can never have enough fragrant ferns, costmary, lily of the valley, moonflowers, nicotiana, day lilies, sweet yarrow, gas plants, peonies, lavender, and roses (can you tell they're my favorite?).

WAKE-UP HERBS. When your bedroom needs a lift, tie fresh-picked herbs to the bedposts or headboard using narrow satin or grosgrain ribbons. The effect is fleeting—the bouquets will wilt in a day—but the herbs' soft greenery and delicate fragrance make the effort worthwhile. To freshen up your sheets and pillows before you make the bed in the morning, spritz them with rose-petal water or cologne.

A SCENTED FIRE. Another thing I really like is a fire in the fireplace. A fire appeals to all the

senses. It not only smells great, but also looks and sounds good, too. Sit back with a glass of hot apple cider and a good book, and enjoy the show!

Fruitwoods make the most aromatic fire, and don't produce smoke. When applewood burns, you'd swear you were standing in the middle of an orchard. Its flames have a rainbow hue. For more beautiful aromas, try avocado, cherry, lemon, mulberry, orange, peach, pear, persimmon, and plum. Fruitwood isn't always easy to come by, so you may need to leaf through your phone book for a firewood supplier. If you have a ready source, consider yourself lucky.

Herbs and spices have their own distinctive, though fleeting, fragrance when burned. Orange peels, cinnamon sticks (presoaked in water for a day so that they retain their fullest fragrance and burn slowly), and bundles of rosemary and lavender are a few of my favorites. Fruitwoods and hardwoods such as beech, dogwood, hickory, locust, maple, mesquite, and oak have an added sensory benefit. They produce glowing coals, the heart of a romantic fire.

All it takes to start a fire is some kindling and a match, but why not embellish from there? To set the stage for fragrant fires, top a stack of firewood with bundles of pepper berries, cinnamon sticks, and fresh-picked herbs. The bundles are tied with thick raffia knots, ready to be tossed into the flames. Not only do the bundles look gorgeous, but they also smell great as they burn.

Burning aromatic woods and herbs in a kettle grill, with a pan of water to create steam and smoke, will flavor and tenderize the foods you're cooking, and captivate the chef in the process.

Personally, I like noisy, shoot-'em-up fires that snap, crackle, and pop. Here in California, we burn eucalyptus, juniper, and piñon to get that effect. These woods spark even when dry and well seasoned. The reason: the mini-explosions of gases from burning resins, pitch, and oils inside the wood. In other parts of the country, try birch, chestnut, balsam fir, larch, pine, poplar, and spruce for the same kind of lively fire that I remember at campfires when I was a girl.

For a colorful fire, toss salt on the flames to intensify their sunny hue. Or treat yourself to items embedded with chemicals that burn in color, such as compressed logs, wood chips, pinecones, or paraffin cups. We live near the beach, and we love to watch a fire of driftwood burn lavender and blue.

WRITE WITH FRAGRANCE. Pretty paper, pens, and inks make the whole process of writing a pleasure. Whatever you're writing becomes more personal, more interesting, more

SCENT AND THE BRAIN

The sense of smell never operates alone. Smell is so strongly linked to the sense of taste that it's often impossible to separate the two. The nose connects to the body's limbic system, which controls the emotions. Sex, hunger, thirst, and euphoria originate here. Our brains can identify over ten thousand different smells. The sense of smell peaks in middle age, when many of the other body systems are weakening. The sense of smell has the strongest power to bring back memories, emotions, and feelings.

important, even if it's just your grocery list. Lately, I've been using scented inks to write letters, postcards, and invitations—and I've found I can be very creative.

My favorite ink is Bordeaux-colored and smells like tobacco blossom, which has a sweet, flowery aroma. Believe me, it's nothing like cigarettes! I have other inks that smell like amber, orange blossom, violet, and pine, along with two exotic ones, jasmine and sandalwood. Some of the prettiest ones have gold flecks in the ink. The inks are water-based, scented with natural plant essences.

To tell you the truth, these scents are primarily for the pleasure of the writer, because the scent doesn't linger long on paper. But the beautiful ink colors do, and are for everyone to enjoy. Who can resist turquoise, sepia, or silver?

I recently enjoyed using the colored inks to write out my daughter's birthday invitations. I pulled a color from the invitations and coordinated my ink. I used bright pink ink that had flecks of gold in it, and even my regular handwriting looked gorgeous. And the elegant presentation took no longer than if I had written them out the regular way.

I've done dinner party invitations in fruit-

scented ink, written place cards in orange blossom ink to match my flowers, and used orchid-scented white ink on the pages of my old scrapbook. You can also match inks to your stationery. Use an eyedropper to add two drops of gum arabic to your bottle of ink. This gives it body and gloss, helping it to bond to the paper and flow from the pen.

Scented inks and glass pens are two of my favorite indulgences. When I use them, everything I write looks special. The variety of inks is astounding, a wonderful mix of color and fragrance. Each pen is a one-of-a-kind work of art. I keep my pens and inks handy for daily use instead of hiding them in a drawer where they might be forgotten.

GLASS PENS. Special inks require a special pen, and when I discovered glass pens a few years ago on a trip to Italy, I knew I had made a perfect match. Now I have two glass pens I'm dearly attached to, and I get a double whammy of pleasure using the scented inks.

Because they are so beautiful, I keep the ink bottles and the pens on my desktop—my real desk, not my virtual one!—and the setup is like a little piece of art. I love to look at all the ink bottles with their labels from different places around the world or pick up a pen and feel its weight in my hand. A bottle of ink is nice to buy in your travels; it's inexpensive to bring home, and makes a wonderful gift.

My favorite glass pens are handblown in Italy. These pens were popular throughout Europe during the Victorian era, primarily because metal was so expensive. It's easy to see why they have continued in favor. My pens are delicate, fragile, and feminine, although they also make weightier ones. I use my pens for writing, but an architect friend says they're great for drafting and sketching as well.

These pens cost from $35 to $200, depending on the complexity of the design and the

Instead of lighting the oven, light scented candles. Everyone will think you've spent all morning toiling in the kitchen. These squat, frosty candles, fragranced with cinnamon, apple, and vanilla, will flavor your house with a heavenly air—even if your pie came from the bakery. Good-smelling candles like these can be delivered to your house by mail once a month.

type of glass they're made of. The pens can be as simple as a plain glass tube, or as fancy as a pen of colored swirls intricately swirled with gold. I've found the less-expensive pens often write just as beautifully as the more-expensive ones do, although they're often not as decorative.

You don't need any experience to use a glass pen. As with a calligraphy pen, you just pick it up, dip it in ink, and start writing. Each pen is all glass from end to end; you write with the faceted end (or nib). The facets hold the ink. The deeper the facet, the more ink the pen will hold; the ink flows with a capillary effect. You still have to dip your pen in ink every three or four sentences, but that's the old-fashioned fun of it. Because each pen is handblown, each nib is faceted in a slightly different way. Some pens create thin lines; others write more thickly. Also, depending on the nib, some pens write more comfortably than others do.

When you're buying a pen, be sure to ask the shopkeeper if you can try writing with it first. Find a pen that writes smoothly and rests easily in your hand. Clean it with luke-warm water or brush it gently with a soft

Imagination can trigger the senses just as surely as the real thing. In this powder room, the scent of pears is evoked by bursting topiaries and a dish of plump speckled soaps. By chance, the posy design on the tiled backsplash mirrors the topiaries' shape—one of those accidental but beautiful pairings that make decorating so much fun.

69

toothbrush if the ink dries on the pen.

The nibs are fragile, so instead of standing them up, lay the pens down horizontally on the desk. I lay mine on a special holder resembling a chopsticks holder. If you happen to break the nib of your pen, don't throw it away. The tip can be restored using glass sandpaper, which is available where the pens are sold.

ECHO THE SCENT. Sometimes it's fun to continue a fruit or floral motif in a fabric or wallpaper with a matching aroma in the room.

If your curtains are printed with lilacs, complement them with a vase of real lilacs on your coffee table. If your kitchen chair cushions have lemons on them, decorate the kitchen table with a bowl of real or papier-mâché lemons.

Bring a home-baked aroma to the kitchen with a candle centerpiece scented with apple, cinnamon, or vanilla, or a mix of all three. Your house will smell like an inviting country kitchen, whether you're baking an apple pie or not. Boil a pot of mulling spices on the stove for the same effect.

MY SCENTED PINECONES. I always welcome guests during the holiday seasons with a big basket of scented pinecones in my entry. Add natural oils to the pinecones to give them a long-lasting aroma, or buy pinecones that have already been scented.

BALSAM PILLOWS. To evoke a winter's day regardless of the weather, tuck tiny balsam pillows behind your sofa pillows—they'll release their scent when compressed.

FRAGRANT TOPIARIES. My friend Leelee makes the most beautiful topiaries. She glues freeze-dried flowers and fruits on Styrofoam balls, and then connects them with painted dowels. She has a lavender topiary in her kitchen, stamping the whole room with the fragrance of the South of France. In her powder room, she continues her creative theme with a topiary totally covered with artificial pears. But what do I admire the most about Leelee's topiaries? They look like her. And that's the objective—making a home a mirror of your soul.

BURIED TREASURE. Long ago, tobacco and black pepper were sprinkled under a rug to discourage moths. Today, cedar sprigs do the same thing. Sprinkle lavender buds on top of a rug. Step on the buds and then vacuum them up, and they release their lavender aroma. Tuck bags of lavender buds between your mattress and box spring to get the same effect.

Layer a room with scent by alluding to fragrance wherever you can. These dried fruit topiaries are studded with cinnamon sticks, pomegranates, oranges, and star anise. Their urns are painted with a verd antique finish. Gold ribbons accent the gold picture frame. All topiaries seem to look best when arranged in pairs, or in multiples of two, so be sure to buy more than one.

SCENT YOUR CLOSETS. Your linen closets take on the gentle scent of spring when you lay lavender stems between the sheets (be sure to leave the buds attached), or when you place a bowl of calycanthus blossoms on a shelf. Calycanthus is an old-fashioned strawberry shrub; pick the fragrant flowers when they bloom in the spring.

Unlit scented candles and unwrapped soaps will also perfume closets, as will minisachets of fragrant herbs tied in light cotton bags.

Two of my all-time favorites are scented shoe stuffers and fragrant drawer liners. Don't confine your drawer liners to your drawers, you can use them under your mattress, or under an area rug. Every time you walk on your rug, they release your favorite scent. It makes good sense!

MATCH A SCENT TO YOUR MOOD. If I want to feel energized, I light a peppermint candle, chew a peppermint candy, or use a calming peppermint lotion on my temples. When I smell lavender, vanilla, or rose, I calm down. Evian water spray or even Sea Breeze, the refreshing astringent I remember from my teen years, makes me feel clean.

Beneath area rugs and small carpets, lay a padding of scented paper—the kind that usually lines drawers and shelves. When you walk across the rug, the pressure of your feet will release the paper's perfume. Drawer liners also make wonderful wrapping paper, place mats, or embellishments for serving trays.

It's refreshing to find fragrance in unexpected places. Tiny bouquets set in silver cigarette holders can scent linen cupboards, kitchen cabinets, or a medicine cabinet. In this glass-front cabinet filled with fancy goblets, a nosegay sits on each shelf. The flowers can be enjoyed whether the door is open or closed. The bouquets are replaced once or twice a week. African violets, primroses, or potted lilies of the valley would work just as well.

Candles
and Incense

CANDLE BOUQUETS. Candles are enchanting. They give your home style, personality, and attitude. When you entertain, set candles on shelves, end tables, and coffee tables—wherever you need an accent.

Instead of a bouquet of flowers, make a bouquet of scented candles for the table. Cluster several candles together, and mingle them with family photos to personalize the effect. This colorful "arrangement" lasts for months, and can be used again and again, filling the room with a subtle scent.

THE DOUBLING EFFECT. An intriguing "doubling" effect intensifies the glitter of your candles when you set them in front of a mirror, surrounded by pieces of shimmering crystal and decorative glass. Mirrored mantels, walls, and trays

Scented candles can take the place of flowers. Combine the scents, like ingredients in a recipe, to create a pleasing combination. These fragrant silver candles look as fresh as mint juleps. They give off a cloud of scent whether they're lit or not—a sure sign of quality. Gala apples become objets d'art when stacked in a clear glass vase.

In a draft, candles burn unevenly and drip. If that's not the look you're after, move your candles out of the wind.

For a pillar candle that will always keep its shape, never drip, and burn to its fullest potential, heed this advice. . . . The first time you burn a pillar candle, don't blow the flame out until the pool of wax reaches the outer edge. Let the wax cool and harden before lighting the candle again. If you blow it out too soon, the candle will never exceed the diameter of the first lighting when it's lit again—and you won't get the most out of your candle.

To loosen candle wax, place candlesticks or votive cups in the freezer for several hours. The wax will shrink and break away cleanly. Then, wash them right in your dishwasher to make them sparkle!

continue the illusion, along with gold, silver, or glass candlesticks, and metallic ribbons and foils. I like to wash glassware and mirrors with ammonia and water to bring out their sparkle and shine.

A CANDLE WARDROBE. If you love candles as much as I do, start a candle collection. I've been buying candles for several years now, and I always search the stores for new scents and unusual colors.

I burn a particular fragrance every month. I call it my "candle of the month." In July, it's root beer, October is spiced apple, November is pumpkin pie, and December is pine. Coordinate your candles with the season.

Candles of the month make fabulous gifts, too! A number of candle companies will be happy to send out candles every month to your friends. It's the gift that keeps on giving—and smelling great!

MAKE HERB-CRUSTED CANDLES. Chunky herb-and-spice-coated candles look intriguing, smell good, and make great hostess or teacher gifts. They can be wrapped with ribbon, handmade paper, or textured sheets of abaca. Smear the outside of the candle with a light layer of craft glue, and roll the candles in a mix of herbs and spices—chosen for their body and dimension. Star anise and the calendula flowers used for herbal tea work well. Cinnamon smells good, but tends to look

Every time you place something in front of the mirror, you take advantage of the doubling effect—a mirror's ability to amplify. This cluster of candles on a dining room sideboard gets a jolt of extra wattage, set on a silver tray near a gilded looking glass. The candle glow is reflected in the lampshades, which coordinate with the wallpaper.

Incense vaults from the hippie category into more elegant realms when burned in a fancy container. In this living room, a trail of smoke rises from a sinuous coil of peppermint incense laid in the hollow of a cut-crystal bowl. The bowl could just as easily be a sparkling vase or a gleaming silver tray. Incense adds a layer of mysterious interest to a room with no effort at all. Just light the incense, blow out the flame, and let the incense smolder. Even after the incense has consumed itself, its scent will linger in the air like a memory.

muddy. These chunky candles give off a homey smell when burned, and everyone likes to run their hands across the candles' bumpy surface.

LIGHT CANDLES EVERY NIGHT. Candles aren't just for company. Lighting candles at dinner reminds everyone in the family that they're just as important as guests!

INCENSE, AS OLD AS TIME. Rediscover incense, twenty-first-century-style. It's as old as time, and was often burned to appease the gods. Nowadays, our concerns are far less weighty—we just want our homes to smell good.

Today's most popular forms of incense (burning sticks, smoldering wands, and perfumed cones and coils) are scented with clean, fresh fragrances such as cedar, sage, and bitter orange. Burn incense in your prettiest crystal bowl or in a pottery holder. Sticks will also burn upright in a pot of sand or in a holder made especially for them.

I like to burn pine incense on my porch a few hours before guests arrive. The breeze diffuses the scent, leaving just a hint of smoky fragrance in the air. Flying insects will be deterred by tall, tapered burn-sticks scented with lavender, citronella, and pennyroyal. It's disagreeable to them, but enjoyable to you and me. Essential oils of lavender and citrus or herbs such as santolina, pennyroyal, or lemon thyme should also do the trick.

Back to Basics

In a world awash with artificial fragrances, it's nice to come across products that smell good naturally.

I'm thinking of butcher's wax for wood floors, lemon furniture oil, cedar chips that absorb moisture and refresh closets. And lavender Castile liquid soap that I use to wash my hands, face, and even my apples. You may laugh, but I've grown unaccountably attached to an Italian glue that smells like almonds and comes in a beautiful canister. You can't eat it, but it smells as if you could. I use the paste when I make scrapbooks and photo albums.

Having said all that, I have to tell you about my sister's napkins. I was visiting her recently, and I noticed that her cloth napkins smelled great. She told me it is because she uses fabric softener. Now she's made me a convert. I'm not brand-loyal—I try all the scents.

I like things with an Asian feeling. These Imari incense pots have just the right amount of detailing to suit my style. I've collected Imari pots for the past six years. I first came upon them in a wonderful New Jersey antique shop and fell in love with their colors. Some of my pots are more than one hundred years old. Each one can hold a single flower stem, a stick of incense, or a stalk of herbs. Grouped together, the pots make an interesting arrangement because each one is a different size. I like to showcase my incense pots on a polished tray, so it's easy to move the setup from room to room.

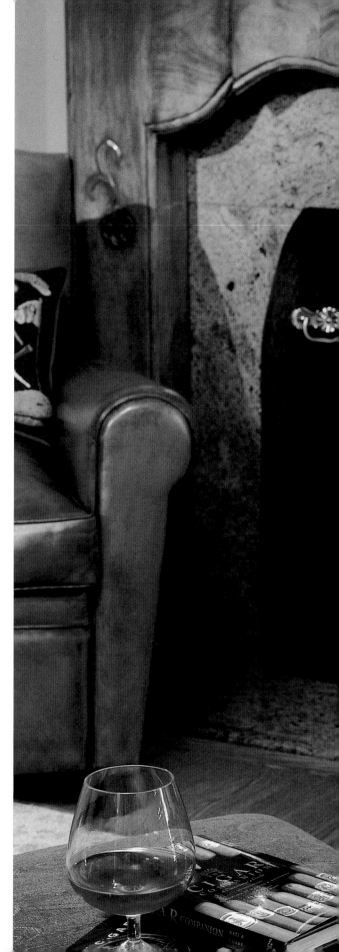

CLEAR THE AIR. The nineteenth-century French poet Charles Baudelaire said, "There is no such thing as a bad smell." But there are times when the air needs to be freshened.

If I'm cooking fish, for example, I burn eucalyptus candles, or clear the air with one of the many sensory air sprays now on the market. Therapy air sprays create better breathing spaces and transform the atmosphere. In short, they just make you feel good.

One of my favorite candles is "The Neutralizer." It eliminates (not just covers) those unpleasant cooking and pet odors, and stale smoke.

To clear the air, there's nothing like the natural smell of fresh-cut lemons. Sometimes, the most simple things can add a pleasant fragrance to your life.

A burning candle clears the air. A candle is especially useful in a room where people are smoking, in the kitchen when you're cooking fish, or in a powder room when you have guests. Any candle will do the job, but some are specially formulated to eliminate persistent or difficult odors like tobacco.

Devils can be driven out of the heart by the touch of a hand on a hand, or a mouth on a mouth.
—TENNESSEE WILLIAMS, *THE MILK TRAIN DOESN'T STOP HERE ANYMORE*

Designing for the Sense of
TOUCH

Touch is the most intimate, affectionate sense.

It helps us enjoy the world. A soft piece of fabric, the

morning sun, cool water in a backyard pool—all these sen-

sations are experienced through touch. Humans can survive

without hearing, sight, smell—even without the pleasures of

taste. But without touch, we cannot survive psychologically.

As researchers continue to unlock the secrets of the brain,

their discoveries continue to confirm the need for sensory

stimulation in our lives. It makes sense to apply this

knowledge to the places where we live. Always include

touch in your decorating equation.

TOUCH DETERMINES THE SPIRIT OF A ROOM.
Every room has a personality. The question is,
Does the "touch" of your room match the
emotion you want it to convey?

Often the "touch" of a room gives it its
definitive personality. Just as a haunted house
scares folks away with its cobwebs and broken
windows, a comfortable home welcomes its
guests with a plush pile rug and an overstuffed
sofa. An exciting, upbeat room might have a
sisal rug underfoot and a zebra-print velvet
sofa. In a feminine room, a needlepoint rug
and a satin chaise are a touching combination.
Velvet and brocade establish a formal feeling,
while glazed chintz or washed denims feel
casual and inviting against your skin.

If a room doesn't feel the way you want it to,
try an infusion of touchable things. When you
suit a room's personality, space comes alive!

**Take advantage of a bay window by nestling
a bench into its cove. To ensure a comfortable
place to sit, this black bench is cushioned in
a quilted minicheck, and shows off dainty
spindles and a back splat painted with a
delicate rose motif. To soften its contours,
favorite pillows are tucked in the corners of
the bench; the smallest pillow extols the
virtues of the old-fashioned button box. A
place to sit isn't quite complete without a
cozy throw, and this plaid chenille blanket has
all the right attributes: a generous size, soft
texture, and a wonderful mix of colors.**

Fabrics
and Textures

THE MAGIC OF FABRIC. Fabrics say a lot about the look and style of your room, but choosing them can be overwhelming. I have a few hints to pass along that will simplify the process.

Believe it or not, I rarely look for fabric for a specific piece of furniture. Instead of shopping like a missile seeking its target ("I need gray velvet for my sofa"), take a freer approach at first. Be an octopus, picking out lots of different fabrics you would love to have in your house — a neutral, a plaid, a stripe, a color, a texture.

EDIT, EDIT, AND EDIT. Only then do you start to edit. Keep only fabrics you love. If you like it, but don't love it, it doesn't make the cut. Don't get carried away by a pretty fabric that's not really you. Have your theme or color in mind as you edit.

Start with colors and patterns you're comfortable with, and build from there. Attach things as you go along that are a little more exciting, a little more outgoing, rather than starting with something garish and having nowhere to go with it. Throw a paisley or a faux ponyskin on your pile without worrying about where you're going to use it.

Then decide which fabric goes on which piece of furniture. You might say, "I really love this paisley, but it would be too much on a sofa, so I'll do it on a chair or a seat cushion." Since you're still in the planning stages, the ponyskin may end up on a footstool—not your sofa. But you won't have to live without it.

COMFORT IS MORE THAN

SKIN DEEP. Comfortable furniture begins from the inside out. When friends sink into your sofa and never want to leave, it's because the inside of the sofa is put together as carefully as the outside.

When you choose a sofa, look for eight-way hand-tied coil springs for comfort and support. I like all-natural materials inside, like jute, muslin, and cotton batting. Cushions filled with 100 percent goose down feel plump and luxurious, and are the most expensive. A less expensive alternative is a combination of down and foam, with the down surrounding a foam core.

Nowadays, the sofa is the family nest, so I always cover it with a soft, durable fabric such as cotton chintz, velvet, a cotton-linen blend, or chenille.

SURROUND YOURSELF WITH

TOUCH OBJECTS. I always make sure my clients have a touchable environment, but it's the one sense I tend to forget about in my own life. This year I'm making a concerted effort to surround myself with things that feel nice, like cut-velvet pillows, inlaid boxes, smooth stones, and, recently, seed balls.

I've seen seed balls advertised in a number of catalogs, but you can easily and creatively make them yourself. The balls are made of Styrofoam covered with glue and tactile beans and seeds. You can use sesame seeds, black beans, white beans, mini-pinto beans, or split peas. I keep mine in a glass hurricane lantern, and I always have a few seed balls on the side. Everyone stops to give them a touch!

A topographic globe gets the same reaction in a client's living room. Guests invariably head over to twirl the globe and run their hands over the mountain ranges.

Beaded velvet fruit is fun and glittery; no wonder it's made such a comeback. These tiny, glittery "brights" (so popular in Victorian times) fit right in the palm of your hand. A glass bowl piled high with beaded fruit can be a centerpiece for the dining-room table. Or place a fruit at each place setting. It will be touched and admired on a bedside table, on bathroom shelves, or in the foyer—anywhere people pause.

Send a kaleidoscope of "touch" messages to the brain by topping a bed, window seat, chair, or sofa with a mix of textured pillows. I

This garden room boasts a soaring ceiling and limestone floors. Its palm trees, casual furniture, and the bird hanging from a lofty perch blur the line between indoors and out. On the wall, Hawaiian prints show the germination of exotic plants step by step. Notice how the ottoman cushions are anchored by long ties extending to opposite feet.

recently saw an interesting pillow made from woven strips of thinnest leather. Polarfleece pillows are nice to cuddle with. Stroking a crewel pillow or a beaded pillow can be mesmerizing, and a small, jeweled pillow reflects light and looks like a precious brooch dropped in your midst.

TOUCH CONTRASTS. I like pairing unexpected fabrics: silks and wovens, wool and gingham, mohair and chenille. I call these "touch contrasts," and they delight the fingers as well as the eyes. Marry a flat cotton with a rough linen, or mix luxurious taffeta with old woven tapestries, or tweed pillows with lace curtains.

When your curtains are of a substantial fabric, such as velvet or brocade, you can achieve

Fluffing a pillow. . . hugging it to your chest. . . propping your book on a pillow in your lap. Pillows are literally the finishing "touch" for any room. A pillow softens the shape of a sofa or chair with a bit of pleasing plumpness, and makes a comfortable seat even more inviting. Choose daring pillows instead of matching ones. Spin off a wallpaper color, a fabric pattern, or choose a vibrant surprise color with dazzling texture. Bring the outdoors in with today's beautiful flora and fauna pillows. Consider wool needlepoint and petit point pillows that sport designs of everything from water lilies and roses, to fish, birds, squirrels, and canine friends. These needlepoint pillows repeat the sofa's floral motif, while the prim striped-silk pillow shares its colors. Each pillow is jazzed up by a border of decorative trim.

91

a striking contrast by hanging sheers behind them—floaty panels underneath that are as light as butterfly wings.

You can double the interest of any curtain by trimming the leading edge with fringe, decorative cloth tape, or beads. (The leading edges are the ones that join in the center when you draw the curtains closed.) Or trim the

leading edges in a contrasting color for visual interest.

Embellish furniture with braid, cord, or rosettes so your fingers can appreciate the openwork, twists, and detailing. You may want to add nailheads to set up a cool counterpoint to the upholstery.

FABRIC SETS A SOFT MOOD. Whenever a room seems cold and uninviting because there are too many hard surfaces, think fabric! One side of my family room is wall-to-wall oak cabinets, thirteen feet wide. To soften the look of all that wood, I cut out the raised panels along the base of the wall unit. I replaced the wood with shirred fabric, and covered the fabric with a woven wire grille (see the Source Guide). Window curtains made of the same hollyhock fabric tie the room together. I was a bit apprehensive about cutting the raised panels from the cabinets. Obviously, there was no turning back! But I trusted my instincts with this idea, and it turned out better than I ever expected!

As you travel and shop, look for a piece of touchable art to put somewhere in your house. A well-traveled part of the house is best, like a dining room, family room, or foyer. The piece serves as an icebreaker, igniting conversation and stimulating the decor. This unusual globe abstractly depicts the continents floating in a verdigris sea. It never fails to draw attention and admiring strokes from anyone who walks by.

Magnify the beauty of your curtains by adding trim to the leading edge. Make simple panels much more decorative with wide bands of solid color, a contrasting pattern, or a beguiling two-tone braid. The color of the trim can either match or contrast with the curtains. These French cotton panels get some cha-cha-cha from an edging of tasseled fringe and clay beads. The trim emphasizes the fabric's vertical pattern.

OLD SILVER. I love old things that are kissed by time, their rough edges softened by history. I recently bought some restaurant silver that used to grace the dining tables of a transatlantic steamship liner. The silver is beautifully worn with age and has a nice heft in the hand. Because it is silver-plated, it is less expensive than sterling.

I love this silver because it's unique—and I suppose that's my point. If I bought a new set of silver, it wouldn't mean as much to me. Oftentimes the choices in your home that are a bit daring and push your creative envelope become your most treasured pieces.

TREAT YOURSELF TO A GREAT MATTRESS AND GREAT SHEETS. A mattress isn't very exciting, but when you find one that provides comfort and support, you'll always wake up refreshed.

> **The hardware that accentuates your upholstery is just as important as the fabric itself. Nailheads are a tactile trim for furniture, outlining special details and tempting your fingers to trace a path. Historically, nailheads were often paired with needlepoint and tapestry. This open armchair boasts a high touch quotient, with its carved wooden frame and needlepoint upholstery; nailheads underscore its shape.**

TOUCH AND THE BRAIN

The skin is densely packed with nerves, or sensory receptors, each with a particular job to do. Certain receptors respond to texture, deciding if an object is rough or smooth. Some receptors sense if something is hard or soft, while others are on the alert for wet or dry sensations. The information is sent along neuron pathways to the brain. Strong sensations send faster and more frequent signals than weaker sensations do.

A choice of mattress and bed definitely isn't a place to cut corners. Your bedroom—probably more than any other room in your home—should look and feel like you. It's a room you should be proud to walk into every night of your life.

It's worth it to drag your partner down to the mattress store and "play house." Buying a mattress is purely subjective; what is "firm" to one person may be "soft" to another. It probably won't be your most memorable Friday night out-on-the-town, but your muscles and bones will thank you for it!

Your skin is the body's largest organ, and when your skin feels good, you feel good. As the old saying goes, we spend a third of our lives in one place—our bed! So when you buy sheets for comfort, be sure you know what you're getting. Contrary to popular opinion, it's not the thread count that is most important, it's the quality of the thread. Thread count is defined by how many threads there are per square inch. One of the best threads is Egyptian cotton, and the thread count may be a mere 210. I'd prefer these sheets over a domestic cotton with a greater thread count any day of the week.

Often I've heard clients say they only bring out their "special" pillows or bedcovers for

Combining floral chintz with chicken wire is a very English thing to do. It was the perfect way to warm up this wall unit. After the unit was built, it was clear there was too much wood in the room. The solution: Lower door panels were replaced with chicken wire, and the chicken wire was backed by shirred chintz fabric that matches the curtains in the family room. This was just enough of a change to make thirteen feet of wooden shelves, cupboards, and drawers more human and inviting.

A medley of plush surfaces brings ultimate softness to a bedroom. An upholstered headboard is much more comfortable than a plain wood one, especially when it's bolstered by a batch of soft pillows. It's easy to mix several different prints in one room if the patterns are small in scale. In this bedroom, the colors in the rose-patterned quilt are repeated in the assortment of print pillows. Everything is freshened by a healthy dose of white piqué.

parties. My advice is that you have a party every night. You deserve the best!

MAKE A TACTILE BED. I couldn't sleep on satin sheets every night, but a friend of mine has them in her guest room. When I visit her, I love sinking into a totally different kind of luxury than I'm used to at home. Crisp oxford-cloth sheets or cozy flannels may be more your style. Find some bedding that suits you—and make your bedroom a more touchable place.

MAKE TIME FOR MASSAGE. On a firm surface somewhere in your house, set up a massage area, with a cloth-covered mat and low lights.

Relieve the body of tension and stress as you relax cold, tense muscles with grape seed, almond, or jojoba massage oils rubbed into the skin. Indulge yourself with a book or a class on massage. Invite your partner to come along!

The formula for creating a comfort zone is easy: a multitude of touchable things and lots of plants and flowers. This bedroom is a nest, with its lacy openwork blanket cover and a headboard banked with pillows. Ivy and flowers add a touch of life, and more flowers burst from the room's upholstered wall panels.

Air

and Water

MOVE THE AIR. When you enter a room, the first thing that touches you is the air, an invisible but powerful presence. Sometimes improving a room's ventilation makes more of an impact than tinkering with the layout or the furniture.

Fans eliminate unnecessary heat and stagnant air buildup by correcting the flow and distribution of air. Air stirred by a ceiling fan is palpable, gently circulating around your body on a hot day. In a bathroom, it's relaxing to dry off under a slowly revolving overhead fan, or watch a mobile bobbing on hidden currents of air from an open window. A lazy table fan slowly oscillating on a desk projects the peace and calm of a library. A portable fan in a

Newer isn't necessarily better. Old things can be a refreshing antidote to "progress." An electric fan, for instance, can be a charming, old-fashioned accent in a world where air conditioners reign. The fan's efficiency just adds to its appeal. This vintage table fan does a marvelous job of cooling off the room, and when it's not twirling, it serves as table sculpture. The bellows hanging on the side of the fireplace is another classic that needs no improvement.

101

kitchen by a window can whisk away smoke just as quickly as a stove's exhaust fan. In winter, reversing the direction of your ceiling fan will warm your rooms, bringing hot air down to living level.

Look for fans in stores, catalogs, and even your attic or garage; antique fans are all the rage, and many companies are reproducing old designs. Today's fans are made of cast iron, steel, or lightest aluminum with blades of plastic, metal, wood—or even canvas or silk. They're made in many diameters to suit the size of your room. Most are designed for eight-foot ceilings, with the blades seven feet from the floor, although extension rods are available for higher ceilings.

Of course, the low-tech, high-touch alternative remains the lowly paper fan, with its graceful Oriental design. A paper fan is a pleasure to touch, as you unfold its crisp pleats into a wide wedge shape. Lay a paper fan on a table as a touchable accessory and watch how many people pick it up to fan their cares away.

Fans are cooling and coquettish. They summon your touch. This trio from Chinatown is rarely at rest. Lay fans on a side table, in a summerhouse, on a porch—wherever people sit and relax. Fans are great as the focal point of a table centerpiece or to decorate bare walls for a party. Translucent fans can be backlit to create a moody atmosphere. Add pizzazz to natural-colored fans by sponge-painting them in bright colors, or spray them gold for the holidays and set them in your Christmas tree.

AIR-CONDITIONING

AND HEATING. Natural ventilation or cross-ventilation is sometimes all you need. But if you need to eliminate stagnant air by moving air around or bringing in fresh air, a ventilation system can be right for you. Clean your air with a HEPA-type filter, which can be purchased at most home stores. A few recommended products on the market are Space Guard Air Cleaner and Second Wind. These items need to be purchased and installed through an air-conditioner company.

When purchasing an air-conditioner system for your home (or a room), be aware of its level of noise. Keep in mind the delicate balance between the "touch" and "hearing" senses in your home.

THE TOUCHABLE TUB. A bath can be so restorative. You can read, relax, and let the warm water nurture your body. A bath pillow and candle are required!

Scenting the water with a pure essential oil turns your tub into an aromatherapy pool, and makes the water feel silky against your skin. For their therapeutic effects, breathe in the fragrant oils, which are distilled from aromatic plants and flowers. Be sure the oil is a pure essential oil; synthetic oils, with their different molecular structure, do not have the same healing effect. Never apply essential oils directly to the skin. To avoid irritation, they should be diluted in water or in a carrier lotion, oil, or balm.

Rosemary oil is uplifting and clears the nose when you have a cold. Jasmine promotes serenity. Ylang-ylang relieves anxiety. Make a soothing compress from a soft washcloth dipped in the scented water, and lay the compress over your forehead, face, or stomach. Smooth a mask over your face to draw impurities from the skin, and emerge with what feels like a whole new skin!

I love the way heavy, old-fashioned tubs hold heat, allowing you to sink past your shoulders and enjoy a long, hot soak. Old tubs are deeper, too. Before replacing an old tub with a new one just because the porcelain is scratched or discolored, consider having it re-porcelainized. It will take on a new feeling.

I recently saw a product that was truly impressive. The "TurboSpa" is a portable whirlpool that you can install in seconds in any tub. It's a great way to enjoy a whirlpool in your bath without investing thousands of dollars in a new tub. I've tried it, and it works as well as any Jacuzzi tub I've experienced. I'm giving one to my brother-in-law for his birthday!

Buy some new bath towels with a texture you're not used to. If you've always bought

Everyday items can be just as charming as grander possessions. Small displays show off your prettiest things, which don't have to be spectacular or expensive. Pastel towels fill this narrow oak bookcase, the orderly stacks offset by a pink enamel clock, a fragrant sachet, and a sunny spray of freesia. The arrangement brightens up a small corner and makes the towels more accessible.

terry cloth, try velour, or vice versa. Stock up on a pile of stimulating waffle-textured massage towels, specially designed to make your skin tingle. And monogram all your towels; no one can resist running their fingers over the letters.

TAKE A ROSE-PETAL BATH. I like to give my girls rose-petal baths—a treat that combines the pleasures of touch, scent, and sight. I gather the petals in my garden, add a few drops of rose-scented oil to the water, and float the petals on top. Use rose petals that have not been sprayed with chemicals. As for the rose oil, it is said to improve everything from impatience to hay fever. Who can argue with that?

THE POWER SHOWER. Over a lifetime, we spend six months standing in the shower!

Rev up your circulation and stimulate the sense of touch with a powerful massaging showerhead and a crunchy loofah body mitt. Wash with a natural sponge and a bar of granular almond-oatmeal soap. Or consider buying

I love beautiful things that are practical, too. This dressing table fits the bill, with its mirrored surface, heart-shaped boudoir chair, silver-backed brush and mirror, and sparkling crystal. The touch treats in the china dish are handmade soaps embedded with multicolored chunks. Besides being great to look at, each soap creates a textured lather that feels wonderful against the skin. Unwrapped, the soaps can be stroked and admired before you use them.

your soap from a shop that makes it by hand in "loaves." They cut the loaves into bars, each embedded with tactile, fragrant things such as orange peel, lemongrass, cinnamon, lime, or poppy seed.

BATHE OUTDOORS. Bathing outdoors is popular in warm-weather climates and at casual beach houses by the sea. Install an outdoor shower near the house, and greet the morning under a blue sky. Find a location where only the birds can spy on you.

A steaming Jacuzzi tub on the deck can be the perfect setting for a party, or as a place for you and your family to have a restful soak at the end of the day.

Turn your bath into an instant spa by making your tub the center of attention. If you're remodeling, position your tub by the window to enjoy a garden view. Or simply hang a painting or a photograph that captures an outdoor scene. Sweet aromas rise from scented candles set in mossy saucers around the perimeter of the tub. These scents mingle with the fragrance of a lavender topiary studded with white hydrangea blossoms. An array of silky bath oils, natural sea sponges, and perfumed soaps set the stage for a well-deserved time-out.

Surfaces

Countertops. Sinks. Wallpaper. Furniture. Many of your home's surfaces are already in place. But when you do have a choice, go for the more touchable material: a soapstone sink, paneling of rough-sawn wood, a cool marble countertop or floor, or wallpaper with a raised design.

Painted walls may be easy to clean, but wallpaper gives a small bathroom or a powder room the feeling of a little hatbox. Touchable suedelike wallpapers or embossed designs can be quite lovely if they're of high quality. Choose wall coverings that make you want to reach out and touch.

If you do decide to paint your wall, use a tactile finish such as sponging, crackle, or striated. Any good painter should be able to show you examples of the different methods.

Aiming for a casual look indoors? Think wicker. Its touch recalls lazy summer days, and it can be woven in all kinds of beautiful patterns. Painted wicker can even be accused of sophistication, especially when an entire room is filled with matching wicker and every piece has a cushion. The cushions on this wicker furniture have a half-inch flange all around. This gives the cushions a tailored look that's more finished than ordinary piping.

111

In furniture, opt for the rough weave of wicker, carved wood at the end of a chair arm, leather upholstery, or a parquet tabletop. The same tactile standards hold for lamps and the frames around pictures and mirrors.

CONTRAST IS KEY. Nature's genius is in its contrast. The glory of a rose is the contrast of its soft, frail petals to its thick and thorny stem. Some of winter's prettiest scenes feature gentle, floating snowflakes against the cold, hard texture of ice. Effective interior design includes the same contrasts. Diverse textures will add punch to your decorating scheme.

BALANCE HARD AND SOFT ELEMENTS. Every room should balance hard elements such as wood, brick, granite, brass, glass, stone, tile, or clay with softer materials. The cold, hard surfaces of a bathroom may seem unforgiving, but the sense of touch is satisfied when you add fabric at the windows, a rug underfoot, fluffy towels, and a shower curtain.

In a foyer, put soft lace pillows on a mahogany bench. On a table, damask napkins glow against the strength of silver and china. Toss an animal-print pillow with black corner tassels on an oversized leather chair. Textured surfaces are more forgiving than shiny ones that reflect dust and imperfections.

BEAUTIFUL HARDWARE IS THE CROWNING GLORY OF YOUR HOUSE. The small details in a house often make the biggest impression. Hardware on doors, windows, furniture, cabinets, sinks, and tubs is more than ornamentation, it's a symbol of permanence, security, and continuity. Fine-quality hardware lasts for years and will always provide sensory pleasure.

As they say, "The first impression is everything." Front doors tell a great deal about not only a house, but also the people in it. The hardware on the door should mirror the drama of your home. Whether it is whimsical, strong, organic, or trendy, the knocker and the handle should capture the essence of your and your home's personality.

To give your kitchen a clean new appearance, just change the hardware; you'll feel as if you got new cabinets! It's a great way to perk up your house inexpensively.

Decide how much hardware you want to show. Different styles often dictate choices you'll want to make in this regard. For contemporary furniture or cabinetry, concealed hinges give a clean look; with traditional cabinetry, you may want to show off the hardware.

In your search for the best and the brightest, don't overlook the ordinary. Mother Nature is famous for her artistry. To make seed balls like these, cover Styrofoam balls with hot glue and attach different colored beans and seeds. When the seeds have dried, lacquer the balls for a shiny finish. These seed balls erupt from a hurricane lamp. The simple shape of the glass magnifies the contours and details of each individual orb.

And stay true to the style and finish of the piece. You can put antique hardware on a modern piece, but the reverse doesn't usually work. Hardware was an indigenous element in the design of eighteenth- and nineteenth-century European and American furniture. As you wouldn't put a modern fender on an antique car, the same is true in furniture design.

Besides the usual specialty retailers, you can buy beautiful hardware from metal artisans like blacksmiths or at shops that specialize in antique hardware. Architects will sometimes design hardware specifically for your needs, creating modern embellishments or taking inspiration from pieces that are centuries old.

Some European manufacturers, including Bouvet and Brionne, have adapted their door hardware for the American market. But, in general, if you're buying a European entrance set, buy the entire set, not just the lock plate. European keyholes are on the bottom, whereas American keyholes are on top, and it's

Special hardware is like jewelry for your house, delighting your hand as well as your eye. It makes your house more personal. Just as you finger a string of pearls or fiddle with a ring, it's a sensory pleasure to feel a cool brass doorknob in your hand or feel the detailing on a beaded drawer pull. This array of antique and new French hardware includes embellishments for doors, drawers, and curtains. Unusual door knockers like the lady's hand with lacy cuff extend an inviting welcome.

impossible to reconcile the "guts" of one with the visible hardware of the other.

Hardware can be hard to describe, so if you see a picture of some that you like, bring it with you when you shop. You may not get an exact duplicate, but it will help the retailer know what you are looking for.

Regular lubrication will increase the life of your hardware; it's something no one does but everyone should do. I use a Teflon spray called Tri-Flow; it comes in a spray can or squeeze bottle. Pick it up at any hardware store.

BUY SOMETHING NEW. Every so often, buy something new to tingle your sense of touch and make your house more comfortable. Cushioned stools. Worry beads. A tulle-skirted dressing table. A slipper chair covered in soft French terry cloth. A plump bed or body pillow. A fluffy comforter or antique quilt. A plant stand topped with a spouting fern that will brush your shoulder with its tender fronds. Make touch a part of your everyday life.

People like to touch things, so give them something to play with. Closets and cupboards often yield fascinating belongings. This chess set is always on display, whether there's a game in progress or not, because the Elizabethan chess pieces and the board are decorative in their own right. If there's not a game in progress, someone is sure to be rearranging the merry band of royals, which has been in the family for years.

music

quiet

ambience

Architecture is frozen music.
—Johann Wolfgang von Goethe

Designing for the Sense of
HEARING

If you want to hear the most beautiful song

ever written in the world, stand out in your backyard

at five-thirty in the morning. It's playing.

Close your eyes and listen to the quiet of life. Every

sound—so clear, so pure and distinct. You'll hear birds

celebrating the arrival of a new day. The wind tugging on

the trees, bending the oak and maple ever so slightly like a

creaky staircase. You can almost hear the flowers and grass

drinking their morning dew. In these rare moments, we

appreciate the beauty of the most musical and poetic of the

senses—the sense of hearing.

Music

Music is like clothing. Without it, a house feels naked. When I come home, the first thing I do is turn on the music; it brings my home to life.

When you listen to music, you're never alone. And you don't have to know a lot about it to enjoy it. Babies in the womb respond to music as early as four months after conception. Racehorses are calmed with music. Even plants seem to grow better when they are serenaded with song.

Like pure emotion, music surges and sighs, rampages or grows quiet. Music can symbolize and mirror our emotions, behaving so much like them it can free us from the nuisance of words. A musical passage can make us cry, or send our blood pressure soaring.

Animate your house by suggesting song as you decorate. Set a pair of rich red conga drums in a corner of your living room. Hang a violin on the wall. Use musical symbols on pillows, rugs, dinnerware, and decorative accents. This set of delicate crystal musicians is light and lyrical. Arranged on a polished tabletop, they provide music for the eyes. They sparkle like a silvery melody. The classical Greek urn behind the figures picks up the color of the instruments—a tiny touch that adds to their beauty.

121

Since my husband is a composer, music plays a big role in our lives, and I feel lucky that my children can share the joy of music with my husband and me. My husband recommends to friends, "The most lasting musical gift you can give your children isn't encouraging them to play music, but to love music. If they love music, they'll naturally want to play it."

Have music fill your home, fill your lives.

MUSIC WITHOUT

SOUND. Having music in the home doesn't necessarily mean owning a piano or a great audio system. You can represent music with lyre-back chairs, lampshades with musical notes on them, plates, figurines, pillows, candles, and trays with a lyrical theme. All these things will wordlessly transmit a sense of music.

GIVE YOUR DAY

ITS OWN SOUNDTRACK. Wake up to classical music, and let it follow you as you enjoy your morning cup of tea, hurry off to work, or carpool the kids to school. Gentle sounds keep everyone on an even keel. Keep a wardrobe of music on hand for other times of the day, and organize it by tempo so you can easily match your mood—or improve it! When I arrived at dance class one morning feeling tired, I found the teacher kicking at the barre to the sounds of Louis Armstrong. It got me moving!

CAR TALK. There's a cozy little room in our lives that is often ignored, even though we spend a great deal of time there—the car. "Decorating" it may just be keeping it clean and clutter-free. With all the time you spend in your car, you want it to be a place you feel comfortable and at home.

Everyone has different places where they love to listen to music. For me, it's in my car, where I'm often alone and can give beautiful music the attention it deserves. I love to roll up the windows, turn up the music, and drive for what seems to be forever. You may prefer a CD changer that can play five CDs continuously from the trunk of your car. I prefer a single CD loader right in my dashboard.

It's the old story: Your system is only as good as its weakest link. Install strong speakers (properly placed) with a strong receiver/radio. I lean toward name-brand manufacturers. Don't get talked into unnecessary gadgets, such as equalizers. Spend your music system allowance on the basics.

LULLABY

AND GOOD NIGHT. Let music lull your children to sleep at night. There's nothing so restful and relaxing. And it familiarizes them with great music in a natural way.

My husband, James, often kisses the girls good night, and then plays them to sleep with gentle lullabies from the grand piano downstairs. One of the pluses of marrying a composer!

PARTY MUSIC. Clients often ask what kind of music they should play for parties. As with all elements of design, your music should sound like your voice, your heart, your soul. Music will then complement your unique and beautiful home.

When friends arrive, you want to focus on them, so program the music ahead of time. Adjust the volume to an appropriate level — not too loud, not too soft — so that conversation is easy. Remember, what's in the air is as important as the food, the flowers, or the decor.

A multidisk (five or more) CD changer is essential to fill a home with quality music. Most CD changers have "shuffle" or "random" modes, which work great for breaking up the music. In this mode, the disks and tracks are shuffled at random, keeping the music fresh and exciting. Also, wonderful, commercial-free programming is available from those small DSS eighteen-inch dish systems. Many cable TV companies offer "cable music" services.

BRING IN THE NOISE. Imagine your house with a big-screen TV or a full-house sound system delivering beautiful music to every room. These items may sound extravagant, but may add thousands of hours of enjoyment to your family's life.

Place audio components where they're most likely to get used — such as in the family room TV/stereo cabinet, a hall closet, or an office. Avoid placing the components too low, where you'll need to bend down to operate them. Also think about ventilation; amplifiers generate a good deal of heat.

Show your passion for music. Use images of favorite instruments in your decorating. These French porcelain plates orbit around a rosebud topiary. The topiary brings out the colors and designs of the plates, as does the white wall they're hung upon. To give this commonplace decorating idea an uncommon slant, unseat the usual symmetry by using an odd number of plates, and a variety of sizes. Displaying plates doesn't preclude using them, either; afterward, the plates easily snap back into their holders and resume their ornamental status.

It's difficult to arrange good storage for videos, cassettes, CDs, DVDs, and laser disks. The optimum situation is storage that is both accessible and hidden. It's worth it to have drawers custom-designed to accommodate your collection. A wonderful touch is adding lighting to the drawers. As with books in a library, the more inviting and organized your videos and CDs are, the more likely they are to be enjoyed.

Place audio components wherever they're easiest to use—in the kitchen, in the front hall closet, in a cupboard in the foyer, in a headboard that has shelves. I've seen my girls calm down and guests relax, soothed by the subtle strains of music, after I put a CD player in the family room.

KEEPING ELECTRONIC EQUIPMENT

IN ITS PLACE. Everyone has so much electronic equipment these days. It's easy to spoil the integrity of a room with an overflow of electronic equipment, which isn't always known for its good looks! Find ways to hide

If you haven't discovered the rapture of rain chimes, what are you waiting for? The chimes in this simple wooden box supply almost an hour of continuous plinking. The sound will keep you company as you read by the fire, and will lull you to sleep at night. Chimes can calm infants, soothe a boisterous group of children, or turn your office into a peaceful oasis. These chimes are a permanent fixture in the bedroom. The nearby bowl of apricots is a direct appeal to the taste buds.

the clutter. This can be as simple as putting your television behind closed doors in an armoire or bookcase, or as elaborate as a viewing screen that disappears into the ceiling when it's not in use.

When you take charge of your equipment, instead of the other way around, your living room remains a living room and your library is still your library, instead of every room resembling Media Central.

If you'd like to hide your stereo, VCR, or cable box behind closed doors or fabric, you can still turn them on with your remote control right from your chair. An "infrared extender device," which you can purchase at higher-end music stores, enables remotes to work equipment not only from behind closed doors, but also from down the hall or in the other room.

KNOW YOUR ENTERTAINMENT SYSTEM. A well-designed system is simple to use. Whether it's a music system, video machines, an entertainment surround system, or video cameras, choose a system with controls you understand. Be realistic. Know your limitations, and know the time you're willing to invest into learning your equipment.

As with your wardrobe, the goal is not to have a lot of clothes, it's to want to wear the clothes a lot. The same is true with entertainment equipment. The only way you'll use anything is if it looks and feels comfortable to you.

For the best view of a big-screen TV, sit back a distance of one and one-half times the width of the screen. If your TV screen is 80 inches wide, your sofa should be at least 120 inches away from the television. With a regular TV, multiply the height of the picture by three. That equation holds true for the new high-definition televisions, which will have wider screens and clearer pictures.

If you'll be watching TV and listening to music in the same room, perhaps your family room, it's possible to have several audio and video remote controls combined into one master remote control. I've seen as many as ten remotes combined into one easy-to-use, programmable "touch screen" remote control. Simplicity comes at a cost—elaborate systems can cost several thousand dollars.

Besides the familiar handheld remotes, remotes can be installed inside walls or on nightstands or tabletops (referred to as keypads). They can be programmed to control everything from indoor and outdoor lighting, security, a spa or Jacuzzi, heating and air-conditioning, retractable drapes, skylights, awnings, closed-circuit cameras for security and child safety, and, last but not least, audio video systems.

As demonstrated in Bill Gates's "home of the future" in Seattle, the day isn't far from when all homes will have the ability to be "smart homes" for a reasonable price. Computers will control our systems, adding convenience, time and cost savings, and more safety and reliability.

HOME THEATER. Home theater is the fastest-growing segment of the home electronics market. Home theater reproduces the movie-going experience in the comfort of your own home.

Home theater has not only become more reasonably priced in recent years, but competition is forcing the systems to improve. The quality and price of a home theater can vary as much as the price of a home.

If you could see behind the projection screen of your local movie theater, you would discover three sets of speakers. The film screen is perforated with millions of tiny holes, allowing the sound to pass through it and to your ears. On the outer edges of the screen, you would notice left and right speakers, reproducing the music sound track or off-screen action. Dead center of the screen you would find the center (channel) speaker. This speaker is responsible for reproducing the dialogue. You'd also find a subwoofer located under the screen, filling out the sound.

Similarly, every good home theater must have left, center, and right speakers, and a

A television is the black hole of decorating when it's not turned on. But thanks to swivel trays and pocket doors, you can hide a television just about anywhere and still see it when you want to. These owners were undeterred by the angle of their wall cupboards. They tucked their television on a sliding swivel tray behind doors that fold away when the set is on. A television can also be hidden behind a standing screen, a curtain, or inside a trunk with a pop-up shelf.

Sometimes things just are what they are. Instead of hiding these remote controls, or losing them between the couch cushions or a pile of magazines, keep them close at hand in a tole cachepot, a container made of French tinware.

subwoofer correctly located along the front of the room, preferably along the same plane as the screen or TV. In addition, "rear" speakers, also known as the "surround channel," are located behind the viewer, on the back or side walls. Ceiling mounting of rear speakers is also an option.

Hiring an audio/video professional can save you time, money, and frustration. To find a qualified audio/video professional, you can contact CEDIA (Custom Electronics Design and Installation Association) at 800-CEDIA-30, or on the Internet at www.cedia.org. Another wonderful resource for A/V-related ideas and information on the Internet is www.poindexters.com.

Choose Your

Speakers Wisely. Imagine a room with the potential of an extraordinary view of the ocean or mountains, with only a tiny window letting in the light and picturesque view.

Often this is the case with music systems and its speakers. A speaker is a window to your musical "view." Old or poor-quality speakers may distort the sound, much like dirty glass in a window distorts or blocks the view.

Speakers are the "voice" of your music sys-

Music provokes and inspires us. America's most famous architect, Frank Lloyd Wright, drafted to Bach and fell asleep to Beethoven. Music was so important to his way of life that he usually had a piano within a few steps of his drafting table.
At Taliesin East, Wright's summer home and studio in Wisconsin, he had speakers installed atop his neighbor's windmill. He wanted the workers tending his fields and remodeling his home to also enjoy the beautiful music he was working to.

tem or television. Buy the best you can afford. Even the most ordinary audio system can be improved by upgrading the speakers, improving their location, or adding a subwoofer.

The young human ear has the ability to hear sounds that measure in the frequency range (response) of 20Hz to 20,000+Hz (or 20kHz). The small, unobtrusive bookshelf or wall-mounted speakers that are currently popular are unable to reproduce the lower frequencies that express the emotion, tension, and excitement found in music. With small speakers, any note two octaves below middle C on the piano (65Hz) will not be heard.

What's the answer? How can you have small, nice-looking speakers with a full, warm sound? Add a subwoofer. A subwoofer takes over where the small speakers leave off, filling out our auditory view of the music. I'd recommend a "powered" subwoofer—it has its own built-in amplifier (engine). It gives realism and punch not only to music recordings, but also to TV sports events, movies, and home video recordings. A subwoofer can be added to any audio system; it's often the answer to making a good-sounding system great.

It doesn't really matter where you put your

Owning lots of electronic equipment doesn't mean your home has to look like mission control. The residents of this house felt a special responsibility to maintain the integrity of its Frank Lloyd Wright design. When they turned the library into a media room, they recessed speakers into the walls. They hid components inside cabinetry, and sensitively incorporated a drop-down television screen and projector in the ceiling. All this equipment disappears when not in use, and the room reverts to a comfortable library.

subwoofer. The best location is in a corner along the same wall as the left and right front speakers.

Similar to the placement of lights in a room, speaker placement can make all the difference. My rule of thumb—music should enter your body in the most "natural" way possible.

"Ear level" is the optimum location for speakers, as it is in recording studios. But placement and dimension of speakers require a balance between form and function. In most cases, corners are best. But don't block your musical "view." Placing sofas in front of floor speakers or books in front of bookshelf speakers is like putting a dresser in front of a window.

Position and space speakers by envisioning a pyramid, with the listener at the top and the speakers to each side, all equidistant from each other, for proper stereo separation.

If you can overlook their size, quality floor-standing speakers deliver the fullest and best sound. Bookshelf speakers and wall-mounted speakers are unobtrusive, but don't transmit the low-frequency range and response so important for music and movie-viewing enjoyment.

Locating speakers in a ceiling is the last

The word "lyric" has its roots in the Latin word "lura" or "lyre," the instrument used in ancient Greece to accompany a reciting poet or a singer. The lyre has adorned furniture and paintings since classical times. This family announces their love of song with a lyre-back chair in the entry. I love the way light from the window casts the lyre's shadow on the wall.

resort. It's unnatural for sound to come from above unless you're in a Wal-Mart or an elevator. Exceptions are sometimes made in kitchens and bathrooms due to space constraints.

Master bathroom speakers are truly wonderful. I've even done speakers inside showers. These waterproof wonders start your day off with a blast. Don't forget the waterproof volume control!

Volume controls are as necessary to a home as light switches and dimmers, and should be placed in each room that receives speakers. In rooms with telephones, it's best to place them close to the phone so the music can be turned down conveniently when the phone rings. In rooms without phones, place the volume control across from the speakers for best results.

How much should you spend? That all depends on your musical palette, budget concerns, and the needs of a room. As with car stereos, I lean toward name-brand speakers—they are often easier to repair if you have problems. As with most items in your home, you get what you pay for.

OUTDOOR SOUND. Music in your backyard or on your deck is something to consider, particularly if you enjoy spending time outside. Outdoor speakers come in many shapes, sizes, and varieties—there are even speakers built to resemble rocks! Many of these speakers are easily camouflaged in a garden, along a fence, or under the eaves of your home. They're especially wonderful for entertaining. But don't forget about the neighbors!

Quiet

ELIMINATE ANNOYING SOUNDS. To create a home that delights your ears, go into each room and listen. For a house that sounds as good as it looks, eliminate annoying noise — and fix anything that drips, squeaks, hums, rattles, or beeps. A leaky faucet, a raucous kitchen appliance, or a cranky air-conditioner or computer fan can unconsciously drain your energy and affect your mood. Refrigerators can generate an enormous amount of noise. Even a few improvements in your home can make a big difference. Something as simple as a bad grounding for cable TV, due to corrosion or a poor installation, can introduce a nasty, unnecessary hum in your music or TV system.

If there are sound problems in your home, you'll hear them loud and clear at night. It's amazing how much quieter it is at night. In

There's nothing like the sound of the sea to relax you. Whether you're calling locally or long-distance, a conch shell is an instant connection to the ocean's echo. Its texture and soft pink gradations of color make the conch shell a triple delight for the senses: it not only sounds good, it looks and feels good, too.

135

Traditionally, designers have been taught to work from the ground up, starting with flooring. And what a wealth of choices there are! These days, what's on the floor is just as exciting as what's in the rest of the room. Textures, patterns, borders, and fringe give today's carpets pep and pizzazz. All-wool carpets, as the ones shown here, last the longest and will look new for years.

they're unlikely to go away. And unless addressed, they will forever be a part of your design landscape and the memory of your home.

For noises you can't do anything about, consider a sound machine. It can re-create the murmur of rain, the surf, or a babbling brook. These handy little boxes mask unwanted sounds, such as garbage trucks, lawn mowers and leaf blowers, traffic, a buzzing saw, or even a snoring spouse. A sound machine can help you go to sleep, lull you as you meditate, or calm you in the office.

REDUCE NOISE

IN THE PLANNING STAGES. If you're lucky enough to be building a house, build noise reduction into your rooms right from the start. In ceilings and inside walls, add a resilient channel, called a Z-channel, between the wood beams and the drywall. This keeps sound from traveling through the structure.

Staggering the studs in the planning stages, putting the studs at different angles instead of parallel, scatters sound, making a room quieter. These studs are not used to support the structure, but are installed alongside the regular studs purely for sound reduction.

Between a first and second floor, install five-eighth inch of lightweight concrete instead of floorboards; the thickness will help to absorb sound. This is normally done in commercial buildings, but works in residential homes as well. The concrete should be poured for the best results, but sometimes it's just not

these hours, you may notice a low murmur in certain rooms of your home. Have an electrician take a look; it's often a wiring problem that can be fixed easily. You may want to invite him late in the day to give him the full effect. But don't ignore this problem. Once you have low humming or buzzing problems,

possible. In this case, use concrete sheets, which are an acceptable shortcut.

Doubling the drywall in a room is another way to significantly reduce noise. The gypsum wallboard panels should be staggered so that the seams do not align. For best results, the seams on the first layer should also be taped and mudded before the second layer is attached.

Double-glazed windows can quiet your house quite effectively. These two plates of glass have an air gap (or argon gap) between them that acts as a buffer, so sound is captured and diffused. A custom option is to angle one of the plates of glass to distort the sound even further. Argon-filled low-E glass can also be ordered for added energy efficiency.

Doors are another concern when you're trying to block sound in or out. Always specify a solid-core door. Also, recaulking door and window frames can help seal out unwanted noise.

CARPET:

THE QUIET FLOOR. I love the softness of carpet. Although it can't be cleaned as well as wood, stone, or tile, it absorbs sound and delivers the ultimate hush. If you find peace in moments of complete quiet, and sometimes seek out rooms where there is no noise at all, cultivate silence in a carpeted room that is yours and yours alone.

Some stores are starting to sell carpet by the square foot, the way homes and rooms are measured, but most carpets are sold by the square yard. Keep this conversion in mind when calculating how much carpet you need, so that you don't overbuy.

For the quietest walk and the richest feeling underfoot, choose a carpet with lots of density. Density helps determine the quality and cost of your carpet. The density of a carpet is measured in ounces per square yard; the more ounces per square yard, the higher the quality, the more it costs, and the more sound it will absorb. The more expensive carpets tend to wear the longest.

Years ago, I took a carpet sample to a dealer who said he could get me the same carpet for less. The carpet sample he showed me looked exactly like the sample in my hand, but after it was installed, it didn't feel the same. I had purchased a different density. I'd shown the dealer five-ounce carpeting and he installed three-ounce; that's why it was less expensive. So now I know. Lower-density carpet may look the same, but it won't wear as well, absorb as much sound, or have the same cushy feeling as high-density carpet.

Heavy wool carpet is my favorite. It looks gorgeous and wears like iron, especially if it is between 10 to 20 percent nylon, which adds strength. Some of my clients are just replacing their wool carpets after twenty years, not necessarily because their carpet is worn out, but because they're ready for a change.

Because wool is a natural material, it expands and contracts with water. Clean a wool carpet with as little water as possible or it may shrink, mat, or pull away from the edges of the room.

Synthetic carpet is less expensive than wool and can give a similar look and hush to a room, but it will never wear or clean as well as wool. If you're buying a synthetic carpet, look for a quality brand name and steer clear of inexpensive ones; they will not last. Synthetic carpets are made in Berbers (a twisted yarn that's looped over), cut piles, and all the traditional loops.

Because synthetic carpets have a lot of air in them, they have a tendency to mat. Install synthetic carpeting over a good 1/2-inch synthetic felted pad to help prevent this. Synthetic carpets used to be plagued by static electricity that attracted dirt like a magnet, but this is no longer a problem, thanks to a special coating that's now added to all synthetic carpeting.

Have wall-to-wall carpeting professionally installed. The cost should be part of your decorating budget, not an afterthought. Hire someone who is experienced, bonded, and insured; this is definitely not a do-it-yourself project.

Before installation, plan the seam layout with your installer. Hide seams under beds or wherever they'll be least noticeable. No matter what anyone tells you, there is no such thing as invisible seams. Ask what equipment will be used. A knee kicker lays the carpet evenly, but be sure a power stretcher is used at the end to pull the carpet extremely taut.

COMMERCIAL CARPET. Home gyms and home offices hardly existed ten years ago; now everyone wants them. Industrial carpet, or commercial carpet, is a smart choice for these busy rooms, and for children's rooms, too—anywhere there is lots of activity and noise. Industrial carpet soaks up sound and is sturdy and durable. It is cost-effective, comes in all colors, and is usually made of nylon, which is easy to clean.

PAD THE FLOOR. Carpet pads are notorious sound buffers. For a firm, quiet walk under flat-profile floor coverings such as sisal, sea grass, coir, or low-profile Berbers, use a synthetic felted pad; the thicker the pad, the more cushion it will provide. Under tufted carpets like loop, cut-pile, or the higher-pile Berbers, use a sponge-rubber pad made of Omalon. Never use Rebond or any pad that contains polyurethane; they produce toxic fumes in a fire.

Let the soothing sounds of nature carry good vibrations through your house. Frank Lloyd Wright, whom many recognize as America's greatest architect, was a master at this mix. His vision for a home extended far beyond four walls. It incorporated the surrounding landscape, roads, ponds, and rivers. At this Frank Lloyd Wright–designed house in California, the terraced outdoor waterfall and fishpond can be enjoyed from inside the house by throwing open tall glass doors leading to the terrace. Wright appreciated the noise and beauty of rushing water, and always designed so indoors and outdoors seemed as one.

Ambience

NATURE'S AMAZING MIXING BOARD. Nature has blessed us with the most amazing gift—a natural "mixing board." It's called our brain. We can stand in a room and bring up or down any sound we'd like. Here's what I mean. Have you ever been in a restaurant, straining to hear what someone is saying at the next table? What do you tell your brain to do? Bring up her voice. Bring down everyone else's voice, and bring down the sounds of the room.

Or imagine standing in your backyard in the quiet of the morning. You can tell your

Bark . . . meow . . . chirp! Pets are unconventional musical instruments. Dogs are the bass, cats are altos, and birds are the sopranos. Pets are a source of endless fascination. They turn up the volume around the house in a way no CD can. For a garden feeling in any room, count on birds. They vitalize the atmosphere with cheerful sonnets and playful antics. They often imitate the trills they hear from birds outdoors. This kitchen's delightful folly is a pair of lively parakeets in a 1920s birdcage, set on a shady brick windowsill. Other noted choristers suitable for the home include finches, cockatiels, and male canaries.

141

mind to bring up the level of the birds, filtering out the annoying mantra of the air-conditioning unit around the side of your house. You'll spot a squirrel climbing up a tree limb. Your brain instantly pulls up that sound of the squirrel's feet scurrying along branches.

Isn't it extraordinary that we're able to do this? Effortlessly and unconsciously, we're doing it all day long.

TUNE IN TO THE SOUNDS

AROUND YOU. Every home has its own personal symphony: the morning prelude of slumbering radiators hissing to life, the everyday overture of ringing telephones and ice popping from the icemaker. Music playing and chili bubbling on the stove. The unexpected interlude of planes overhead, a jackhammer down the street, the wail of a siren, the evening coda when the dishwasher swishes and the kids pad off to bed. We're soothed by the tinkling of wind chimes, flags flapping, a burbling creek, the jingling of a dog's tags, and fountains in a pond.

The key is to blend all the sounds of your life into one harmonious mix that makes you feel excited and invigorated, calm and secure.

GET A NEW

DOORBELL. A doorbell with a crisp, clear tone announces visitors in an upbeat way. Don't settle for a doorbell that's muffled or emits an unpleasant sound. If you have an older home, the doorbell was probably installed years ago and needs updating.

Use outdoor things indoors—it surprises people. Do the opposite of what's expected and new possibilities unfold. Try a stone garden bench in a foyer, flats of grass on the dining room table, bowls of rocks, seashell mosaics, vines climbing indoor walls, and a weathervane atop the bookcase. These minichimes hang inside the kitchen window, broadcasting breezes and eliminating "dead air" with their merry melody. Try copper or porcelain chimes—each has a different tone. Farm-animal chimes animate a country kitchen. Fish chimes swim from the ceiling of the kids' bathroom. No breeze blowing through your house? No problem! Place the chimes where people can provide a tap as they pass by.

The sound of a doorbell is like music, and popular sounds have changed over the years. Today's doorbells come with features like adjustable tone, tempo, and volume, and a choice of preprogrammed tunes. Chime tubes look like outdoor wind chimes and have a similar tone.

CAPTURE THE WIND. When my outdoor wind chimes broke a few months ago, I took them down and forgot all about them. My neighbor mentioned that she and her husband missed hearing the chimes when they sat on their deck. Since then, I've replaced them. I'd forgotten how peaceful they sound.

We expect to hear nature's chorus outdoors, but why not bring it indoors, too? When the wind blows, and even when it whispers, let wind chimes capture every current. Chimes add sparkle and freshness to a room. They're audible air. Hang them by the front or back door, or next to a window in your office or kitchen—anywhere you spend a lot of time.

I put chimes outside our breakfast room window so the whole family can hear them as we eat. I've found chimes for the back of a door that jingle when the door is opened, and tiny desktop chimes that I strum with my finger or a pencil.

Wind chimes make different sounds depending on their shape and material. The mellow ring of tubular metal wind chimes is my favorite. I'm also captivated by Zen rain chimes, which look like bronze cymbals and have a gentle ringing sound.

The sound of chimes is heaven's music. Anywhere there's wind, let the ethereal music of chimes resonate through your home.

MAKE THE MOST OF WATER. There is something about water that moves the human spirit. Recently, I've become fascinated with Japanese indoor rock fountains. A tabletop fountain costs about $100. You just fill it with two cups of water, plug it in, and the water travels over rocks and bamboo with a calm, burbling sound—the water recycling again and again. It's like having a garden fountain indoors.

You can also bring the "outdoors in" by opening your patio doors—inviting in the soothing sounds of your fishpond or fountain from your backyard or patio.

SAIL AWAY WITH A CONCH SHELL. Like a ringing telephone that insists on being answered, a conch shell attracts lots of interested listeners. When you set a beautiful conch shell on the table, who can resist picking it up to listen to the ocean? With a conch shell, the sound of the sea is available to you no matter where you live.

BUY A BIRD. Birds sing one of nature's prettiest songs. If you are ready to handle the demands of a pet, buy a canary, parakeet, or a pair of finches for your house. Outdoors you can set up birdhouses and plant bushes and trees that attract and shelter songbirds. Leave the windows open, and your indoor bird will

answer the outdoor warbles, creating a bird symphony in surround-sound.

IMPROVE

THE ACOUSTICS. Acoustics are one of the most overlooked aspects of room design. In a room with good acoustics, conversation is easy and you can appreciate your surroundings. On the other hand, we've all been stuck in a noisy restaurant or an echoing meeting room, unable to hear what others are saying. The brain goes

The splash of waves on the beach or a babbling brook has soothed man's soul for centuries. An indoor fountain lets you enjoy these same sounds inside. Fountains come in all sizes. Many fountains are small enough to fit on a tabletop. These tabletop fountains don't require special plumbing; just fill with water, plug in, and the gentle water sounds begin. This graceful bamboo fountain makes a calm, burbling sound. Its simple Asian style suits any sort of room. The fountain sits on a bamboo tray near a porcelain ginger jar and a tortoise glass bowl of scenic carved gourds.

on sensory overload, and we feel irritable, confused, and overwhelmed. It's usually not the people in the room that are the problem, but the acoustics.

In the simplest terms, sound is like light—reflected, absorbed, and diffused around a room. Hard surfaces such as plaster, drywall, stone, marble, concrete, tile, and flat wood act like sonic mirrors—they reflect sound much as a mirror reflects light. Soft surfaces such as drapes, carpets, couches, upholstered walls, and closed cell foam absorb sound much as dark colors absorb light.

Improving the acoustics of a room is easier than you think. Blend hard, soft, and irregular surfaces to create a pleasing balance. Usually, a room is too noisy. I've rarely had a client say a room is too quiet. In an echoing room, offset unyielding wood, plaster, tile, stone, and drywall with soft carpeting, curtains and valances, upholstered furniture, and varied surfaces, such as bookshelves. Screens help muffle sounds, as do padded walls, tablecloths, and pillows.

When the balance is right, you'll know it.

WHY I LIKE WOOD FLOORS. I'm a real fan of wood floors, and I always advise them for several reasons. Hardwood floors are easy to clean. They become an extension of the furniture, adding warmth to your home. Yes, they're noisier than carpet, but the sound of heels against a hardwood floor has a grounding effect that makes me feel secure.

Maple floors are my favorite, but like any wood that has little grain, every heel mark shows. Oak is the most popular hardwood floor in the United States. It is durable, relatively inexpensive, and easily stained. I like white oak, which has a prettier, tighter grain than red oak. Beech, ash, and walnut also show their grain and camouflage dirt. Floors made of these woods don't require as much tender loving care.

In our house, the wood floors creak upstairs, and I can't get out of bed and walk down the hall without my children hearing me, even if it's two in the morning. I've never fixed this because the children tell me it makes them feel safe. For the same reason, I never oil my screen door. I like to know when someone is going in or out.

If you're building a house or moving into a house with hardwood floors, don't cover them with carpet right away. Live with them for a while. If you decide your house is too noisy, you can always add carpeting or an area rug later, but you'll have the hardwood underneath. The hardwood is your security base.

I used to put runners on stairs, but now I leave stairs bare unless a client has a sensational runner. In decorating, less is usually more. It's easier to add than to take away; it's more cost-effective, too.

STONE AND TILE. Stone or tile is ideal for the "turning lanes" of a house—the pivotal areas where people move from room to room. You can lay it in giant swaths; in Europe, it's not unusual for stone floors to flow through an

In the past few years, I've noticed my clients asking for wood floors more than ever before. Nothing can compare to the richness and warm sound of a genuine wood floor. Wood floors have come a long way since the early days of this country, when a simple planked floor was typical in most homes. And though plain wood floors are still a beautiful choice, you can also be more creative. Combining different types of wood and laying them in patterns, the floor becomes more of a focal point in the room. The floors shown here, from plain to fancy, are just a few examples of what's happening in wood floors today.

Color gives rhythm to a room just as surely as music can. You can almost hear the rushing water as you step onto this mosaic-tiled bathroom floor where sea creatures reign. Continue the conceit by adding a freestanding fountain somewhere in the room. If you're starting from scratch, build it right into the wall. Or put your antique birdbath to good use by moving it in from the yard as a showstopping decorative element. Instead of filling the birdbath with water, fill it with polished stones, or colored glass stones that match the floor tiles.

entire house. I love the continuity of tile carried indoors from outdoors—from a back patio, through French doors, and into the family room. Or from a front-door entry right into the living room.

Stone and tile are beautiful, durable, and easy to clean. If you're worried about a stone or tile floor feeling cold, install electric coils beneath them when you build. Or top the floor with an area rug.

Stone and tile make a distinctive noise. Limestone, granite, slate, terrazzo, concrete, and brick sound solid and outdoorsy. The tap-tap of marble sounds regal underfoot, while glazed tiles have a contemporary click. Unglazed tiles sound mellower.

Stone or tile floors are a long-term investment. Most likely, they'll be there longer than you will! I like stone or tile in foyers, bathrooms, powder rooms, and kitchens—in fact, they can go anywhere. I have a client whose entire bedroom floor (including the closets) is eight-by-eight natural terra-cotta pavers—and it looks great.

Stone and tile are a feast for the eye. Choosing them is a lot like choosing fabrics—eliminate what you don't really feel passionate about and the right choice will present itself. Here are some other tips to keep in mind as you shop:

• Recall the architecture of your house; stay within the boundaries of that style.

• When choosing tile, decide which is more appealing to you: a solid color or a pattern. Bright-colored tile will excite a space; light-colored tile tends to soothe and makes a small space feel bigger. Tiles with bold, complex patterns look better in larger spaces.

• In high-traffic areas, hide dirt by choosing tile or stone with a bit of variation.

• If you want to see the stone or tile, not the grout, choose smooth-edged stones or tiles. They don't require large grout joints, as irregular-edged stones and tiles do.

• For pizzazz and interest, set tile in unusual ways. Do a running bond, the way bricks are laid, with the tiles offset every other row so the joints don't fall in straight lines. Lay tile on the diagonal to open up a small room. Jazz up inexpensive tile with a different-color border, inset keys, or corners.

• A stone or tile floor should be level with the floor it abuts so that you don't trip going from room to room. A good contractor or installer should take care of this, but keep it in the back of your mind.

• Large stones or tiles tend to be the most cost-effective. They cost more per piece, but are less expensive per square foot. With fewer pieces, installation costs less.

Not everyone can play an instrument, but anyone can ring chimes. Hang some over a doorway to herald arriving friends. Set chimes on a table and no one can resist a strum. These desktop chimes are small enough to fit anywhere. They can be moved from family room to bedroom to kitchen, delighting everyone with their tune. For a decorative touch, the frame of these chimes is wrapped with a trailing strand of ivy.

herbs

fruits

spices

Designing for the Sense of
TASTE

Taste is the most festive sense—"the party sense." Think

of taste, and laughter, good food, and gatherings of people

come to mind. Decorating with taste means extending

yourself, pleasing others, and showing your heart. There's a

sense of occasion when champagne chills in a silver urn,

salad greens sprout on the windowsill, and windows are

draped with deep wine-colored velvet curtains.

Just as new foods broaden our horizons, tasty decorating

opens up new avenues of expression. You can't literally taste

your home, but it should be filled with sights, colors, and

images you crave. If you've ever salivated over a beautiful

room at a show house, or felt hungry looking at walls painted

raspberry red or café au lait, you know what I mean.

THE CANDY DISH THEORY. Start by putting something in each room to tickle the sense of taste. I call this the "candy dish" theory. I like dark-chocolate-covered espresso beans, fresh-baked bread, plates of cookies set out for sampling, jars of lemon drops, and bowls of fancy almonds in black, white, silver, and pastel colors.

Express yourself with favorite candies, hors d'oeuvres, cocktails, desserts, and other "tastes" in the home. I've accented my kitchen with jars of pickled lemons, jams, and bottles of olive oil and herb vinegar. Sometimes I buy oversized versions from food-club warehouses simply as decorations.

Then stir up interest with witty taste accessories like Murano glass "candies" and soaps that resemble petits fours.

To make a series of prints stand out, put them in matching frames and hang them symmetrically. This set of eight juicy fruit botanicals is matted and framed in identical fashion. The gold frames share their sparkle with the buffet's gleaming silver tea set, candlestick lamps, and starry wallpaper.

153

Fool-the-eye surprises make a room come alive. These bonbons look real, their colors as bright as the pottery and sunflowers on the table. But, in truth, all these candies are made of Murano glass. They extend a sweet promise with zero calories. For fun, real peppermints are sometimes mixed in with the fakes. The masquerade is revealed only when you try to unwrap one.

Radishes, mushrooms, walnuts, hard-boiled eggs: celebrate the art of good eating with plates of faux nibbles. In this hallway, nine tempting servings are arrayed above an old garden trellis as a reminder of good things from the garden. The plates could just as easily revolve around a still-life oil painting or a food-related wall sculpture.

If you're going to tile your fireplace, consider handmade tiles painted with china plates, to give the room a tasty accent.

Plates fill space inexpensively, and are a fast way to create a look. Hang plates on the wall, let them lead you up a stairwell, or set them on small Oriental stands inside cabinetry. Plates with special motifs (tomatoes, fish, architecture) tell about your interests. To get a food theme going, hang plates that look like lettuce leaves, or plates topped with faux mushrooms and other fun foods.

Plates aren't just for dining room walls. Hang plates over doorways, and in powder rooms, hallways, and bedrooms. In an exercise room where you're trying to work off the effects of eating, food-motif plates make a merry statement.

Cater to your sense of taste with fabrics and wallpapers. Just as you'd toss a salad, toss a

TASTE AND THE BRAIN

Technically, taste happens when food and saliva mix in the mouth. A chorus rises from buds on the tongue, alerting the brain to the "big four" flavors: sweet, sour, salty, and bitter—and secondary sensations like pungency and astringency. Cells in the nose and throat get in on the act, too, because taste and smell work in tandem. A "taste" is actually 10 percent taste buds, 90 percent aroma.

cotton printed with tarragon and olives with pillows made of a lettuce-print cotton. The wallpaper in my favorite restaurant looks like a blossoming chintz, but close inspection reveals not flowers, but tomato plants! In an elegant setting where a light-hearted approach is unexpected, this sort of surprise always provokes a smile.

Two of my favorite fabrics that always make me salivate are called "Designer's Guild Salsa" from the Osborne and Little's Collection. One fabric is called "Pesto," which has tarragon, basil, and mint leaves covering the fabric. Another is "Limonaia," which shows lemons, limes, and oranges. The Osborne and Little's Collection is available through your interior designer or architect.

As a finishing touch, perfume the air with a flavorful essence. Cinnamon, vanilla, or mulling spices added to lightly boiling water will make you salivate as they scent the house.

INVENTIVE POTPOURRIS. I love to make out-of-the-ordinary potpourris—mixtures that provoke a double take and bombard the senses in new ways. One of my favorites is peppercorn potpourri, because it's nothing like the sweet, perfumed mixtures that have made traditional potpourri a bit passé.

I like dangling orange peels above the stove, where the heat from cooking releases their marvelous tang. In this kitchen, the scent of citrus mingles with the comforting vapors of cinnamon sticks, nutmeg, and cardamom simmering in a pot. The natural green color of the wall tiles is a wonderful choice for a kitchen because green looks great with all foods.

Large quantities spell generosity, especially when it comes to food. In an entry, extend a big welcome with a heaping bowl of white pistachios, and keep a smaller dish handy for discarded shells. This embellished silver loving cup is a suitable mate for the eighteenth-century American porringer.

A bowl of pink peppercorns makes a unique potpourri, particularly in a man's study. To fill a large server like this one, pad the bottom with wadded tissue or packing peanuts, then top with a generous layer of peppercorns.

In contrast, peppercorn potpourri has a decidedly masculine air. To make it, fill a bowl or jar with a variety of colored peppercorns. When you run your fingers through them and sniff the air, you can almost taste the peppers. I like to mix two Indian peppercorns in a clear glass bowl: Tellicherry black and Mysore green. Or stir four colors of peppercorns together, such as Tellicherry black, Mysore green, Muntok white from Java, and Réunion pink (from the French island of Réunion). The pink peppercorns are very striking and make a fine potpourri on their own.

If you love the smell of coffee as I do, blend a coffee bean potpourri. Mix several types of coffee beans in an antique wooden dough bowl, using different roasts in different colors. A bowl of coffee beans costs less than a bowl of conventional potpourri, and is far more inventive. Or use pistachios; if you buy them in bulk, they're an affordable luxury.

For a light spice potpourri that's more visual than anything else, fill a tray with rosemary branches, sweet licorice-scented star anise, and extra-long cinnamon sticks.

I have a bowl of "kitchen potpourri" on my countertop, and I add to it constantly. I dry the citrus peels left over from a baked apple pie and toss them in the potpourri—and shake in cinnamon and nutmeg. I grate lime, orange, and lemon peels over the top every once in a while, turning and stirring every day.

Use a special bowl—maybe a wedding present you've always considered too pretty to use. I don't think you have to keep potpourri covered, as everyone says. Once the fragrance starts to fade, wake it up by adding a few drops of refresher oil. Or rub oil on the skins of dried apples or oranges, and set the fruit in the potpourri for scent. Because food is prepared in the kitchen, I use fruity, sprightly essences instead of cloying, perfumed scents.

MAKE A "SURPRISE DRAWER." I love my friend Shawn's whimsical little taste table with its "surprise drawer"—hidden away in the corner of her living room. The drawer is lined with starry paper and filled with the most delicious wrapped candies imaginable, which are constantly replenished. My girls love going to Auntie Shawn's house to see what's in the drawer! I keep saying I'm going to create one of these special drawers myself. It brings a smile (and a smack) to everyone's lips.

My friend's "surprise drawer" brings back fond memories of visiting Grandma's house as a young girl. After we'd kiss her at the door, we'd all race to her surprise drawer in her dining room secretary. Little did Grandma know she was designing for the sense of taste!

TASTY FURNITURE. Wood is a perfect vehicle for transmitting scent. Rub cinnamon, apple, lime, or vanilla essential oil inside a wooden armoire, dresser, or cupboard, and you'll be greeted with a "taste" of fragrance every time you swing open a drawer or door. Rub the wooden undersides of a chair or sofa for the same effect, avoiding fabric or finished surfaces, which will stain.

WAKE UP A MEAL WITH EDIBLE FLOWERS. You can cast the spell of a garden party over any meal by adding flower petals. If you're eating outdoors, line a garden path with petals, as if fairies were leading the way to your table. Decorate the table with floating flower-shaped candles in shallow dishes of water, and set flower petals adrift in the water, too, as a delicate ruffled edging to each candle. Strew flower heads and petals on the table right before everyone sits down.

Colorful, edible flower petals wake up salads and slaws. When I was a child, my birthday cake always had real flowers on top, and now I decorate my girls' cakes that way, too.

I love using pansy, rose, calendula, and nasturtium petals in my cooking, and in spring, I serve bright yellow squash blossoms fried in a thick corn batter. One caveat: Make sure the petals you eat are not poisonous (most garden books list the ones to avoid), and use only unsprayed flower petals from your own garden. Flowers growing wild may be contaminated with automobile exhaust or toxic sprays.

DECORATING WITH

SPICES AND HERBS. Because I love cinnamon sticks, they're all over my house, like little taste "vignettes." I set them in mugs and flowerpots. I bind lots of them together with twine like a stack of little logs, and set them on my desk or the countertop. You can glue them around a candle or votive and use one at each place setting at the table.

Herbs are so pretty. I use them for much

more than cooking. I always have fresh-cut herbs bundled in the kitchen, ready to snip. Instead of flowers, I often make a small green bouquet of fresh herbs for my desk. When the mint looks lush, tuck two fresh mint leaves around the soap in your soap dish. To make a tub tea, hang a little handkerchief "hammock" filled with citrus zests and fresh herbs from the faucet of your bathtub. I leave a fresh one on the faucet even when I'm not taking a bath, just because it looks so pretty!

When you soak in a hot tub, eat something cold like a citrus pop or a raspberry sorbet to bring all the senses into play. Sprinkle dried herbs under your mattress, in a desk drawer, and inside your pillowcase. Freshen all your rooms, not just the kitchen, with pots of fresh herbs, called *potagers*. I love the way rosemary thrives in a steamy bathroom.

THE ZEST OF

AN ORANGE. Citrus is so appealing that I'm always looking for ways to include it in my decorating. I hang long, curly orange rinds from the exhaust hood over my stove. When I cook, or even when I'm just boiling water, the steam rises, and the peels emit their orange grove scent that lightly perfumes my kitchen.

I like citrus so much that I even use it in my coffee. I use a vegetable peeler or a knife to cut aromatic chips from the skin of a well-washed orange, and bury the shavings in the measured ground coffee in the filter in my coffeemaker. The brewed coffee has a bright, clear taste and fragrance redolent of orange.

PLANT YOUR OWN SALAD BUCKET. A window box brimming with greens looks great in a kitchen, but is even more effective in an unexpected place, such as a bathroom or a home office windowsill. The fresh, fluffy leaves are light refreshment for the eyes. In the right spot, you can raise cilantro, mesclun, kale, spinach, and chervil in warm or cool weather year-round.

Salad window boxes are often sold in kit form, but I like to make little salad buckets of my own by gathering a mix of favorite small lettuces and herbs at the nursery. I plant them in a galvanized bucket, with stones in the bottom for drainage, and pick what I want at dinnertime.

The tang of the Spice Islands fills the house when you use essential oils or herbal furniture oils to flavor your furniture. Rubbed on the edge of cupboard doors, the oil emits a trail of fragrance when the doors are opened or closed. Try the same trick on doorjambs, drawer tracks, or the bottom of a shelf, testing the oil on an unseen area first, to make sure it doesn't stain. We used mouthwatering cinnamon oil on this cupboard, which gives the room a taste of warmth. If you're using an herbal oil especially made for wood furniture and surfaces, it can be spread more liberally, to clean and beautify the wood while leaving behind a wonderful herbal scent.

Visual
Presentation

START A

COLLECTION. Some decorating effects can be created in an instant, while others take a little more time. Collecting is one of those things that take time—in fact, it can take a lifetime! Collections give guests an insight into who you are. They show what's important to you.

If you like food, cooking, or even just eating, collect something related to taste. I think antique copper pots, tea kettles, and colanders look great in a kitchen. The old copper pieces are the best, with their dents, hollows, and wonderful patina. The more beat-up they are, the better. Hanging from a pot rack or over the range, they're an instant piece of artwork, adding color and great warmth.

Some people think collecting is all about

Grow your own salad on a sunny windowsill. Choose three or four tasty seedlings at the nursery. Plant them in a favorite urn. This little dish garden is nestled in a tole container that looks like Napoleon's hat. The collection of 1930s and 1940s salt and pepper shakers is an invitation to spice up your salad.

163

acquisition and display, but I think they miss the point. Collections are important because they evoke memories—of times, people, places. Collecting is not just another way to amass things. It's more than the objects themselves. Your collections are a way to personalize the house—not with little tchotchkes, but with things in good taste.

For fifteen years, I have been collecting little tortoiseshell boxes from all over the world. I know exactly where each one is from. I've received some as gifts from friends and they're a wonderful "symbol" and reminder of our friendship. They sit on my coffee table and I love each and every box. I'll probably never stop collecting them.

Though tortoiseshell boxes are costly, collecting doesn't have to be expensive. I also collect salt and pepper shakers from the 1930s and 1940s that cost between $10 and $25 a set. I have about twenty sets now, and the collection just keeps growing. I get a lot of them for my birthday. People will see them when they travel and say, "Oh, this is great for

Set a well-appointed table to tantalize the senses even before the food arrives. I love a glittery centerpiece that reflects the brilliance from a hanging chandelier. Generate interest by balancing light pieces with heavier things: delicate glassware with your finest silver; crisp linens with sturdy plates. This table benefits from a mix of vintage transferware-brown plates atop red—and cutwork linen place mats and napkins. The centerpiece is Victorian beaded fruit set in a crystal compote.

165

Catherine's birthday, I'm going to buy it now." I keep these in the greenhouse window in my kitchen.

If you don't have a collection, start one. Lots of my clients tell me they're not collectors, but when we look through their houses, all kinds of things appear. Gather anything that shows where you've been, what you love, who you are. That's the start of a great collection.

SET A TASTY TABLE. Let your table settings mirror your personality. Maybe an eclectic collection of scenic transferware best expresses your acquisitive style, all of it lovingly gathered at flea markets, hardware stores, and backyard tag sales. A formal setting of bone china edged in gold may proclaim the real you. Whatever your type, show it in your table setting.

Then use food (and images of food) to amplify the effect. If you want to evoke the outdoors, use banana leaves or grape leaves as coasters and fruits as place card holders. Stick candles into hollowed-out fruits and vegetables, or mound raw fruits and vegetables into a packing crate or pretty basket as a centerpiece. I like to tuck herbs into the fold of a napkin, especially when I'm serving something that features that particular herb. Place mats that look like canning labels are inexpensive, make great Christmas gifts, and last for years. You can buy these by ordering them from the Metropolitan Museum in New York City.

Every so often, edit your possessions and

When you suggest taste in your decorating, your house takes on a new "flavor." Some examples: place mats with a teacup pattern, an antique farm sign on the wall, a watermelon doormat, or tall frosty "drinks" like the ones on this table. The drinks are made by filling glasses with chopped citrus, and topping each one with a floating candle. For the holidays, fill the glasses with cranberries. For a birthday party, try a haystack of colorful candles underwater, and light the floating candle to celebrate the occasion.

weed out weak components. You may have stunning dishes and elegant silver and glassware, but if your table linens are unappealing, the whole effect unravels. Keep only your best things, whatever "best" means to you. And never underestimate the power of simplicity.

FRUIT AND VEGETABLE TOPIARIES. Fresh topiaries are great if you have the time and inclination to tend them, but sometimes you want a fresh effect without any upkeep. Ceramic fruit or vegetable topiaries evoke the sense of taste and inject a surge of color into a room. Ceramic topiaries are no-maintenance and always look good, no matter what the season. For perfect symmetry, I always use topiaries in pairs, setting one on each side of a buffet or mantel. Some of them look so real that they're almost edible.

JUICY INDOOR PLANTS. Drop whole, fresh lemons on the soil of any potted tree or plant to add a welcome spot of color where it's least expected. Bedding the lemons in moss or planting ivy in the soil softens the effect.

LET YOUR COOKING COME OUT OF THE CLOSET. A friend of mine, Jacquie, keeps her cookbooks out for everyone to see, instead of hiding them in a cabinet. She feels cookbooks are so beautiful and the photos are fun to look at. Library stands don't have to be limited to dictionaries; they can be a creative, wonderful home for your favorite cookbook.

FREE HAND. Two crafts, hooked rugs and découpage, can add a delicious dimension to any room in your home by incorporating the combination of flowers and fruits as a theme.

You can learn to make these creative wonders either by taking a class or by buying one of the many available books on these subjects.

GLASS FRUITS. Glass fruits are an elegant and tasty addition to a room. Apples and pears are the most common, and easy to find. Use them as perfect paper weights or a stunning centerpiece on a table. I like to surround a bouquet of fresh flowers with a collage of glass fruits. It's a spectacular juxtaposition of the soft flowers against the hard glass.

Glass fruits always look so beautiful when the sun comes streaming through them.

A great place to display your collection is in the powder room—a very well-traveled place in your home!

TASTY PAINT COLORS. Sometimes it's hard to describe the color that you're imagining for a room to a painter; often food colors are easy to envision. One color I always have success with is coffee with milk. Believe it or not, this mocha shade is highly flattering and very serene. I've used it in living rooms. In one home, I complemented mocha-colored walls with bookshelves in a robin's egg blue—a pleasing combination.

Another favorite of mine is pale butter yellow—just ask my clients. At least one room in any given house I've designed is inevitably in

this color. It's neutral, and pleasingly complements every color nature has rendered. Just
take a stick of butter and tell your painter,
"This color, please." If you find the color is
lighter than you wanted, just scramble some
eggs and go a shade darker.

Buy a pint of your paint color and test it on
your wall before you commit. (Give it twenty-
four hours to dry.) Colors not only change
their tone when they dry, but also often appear
differently than expected against the backdrop
of the rest of the room. Also, be aware that
light permeating a room at different times of
the day will alter the attitude of a room.

TASTE TREES. Something fun for children (and
adults) is to turn an indoor evergreen into a
taste tree. Buy tiny bird's nests at a craft store
and glue them to the branches of your tree. Fill
each nest with a particular berry, seed, spice,
or candy; the whole tree becomes a medley of
taste, color, and texture. Include cranberries,
bay leaves, lavender, cinnamon, cloves, raisins,
cinnamon red hots, chocolate chips, and
anything else you hunger for. Everyone will
love sampling the edible parts of your display.

**Bright collections are a treat for the eye.
Arranging a collection can be just as thrilling as
the hunt itself. It's no surprise that this windfall
of apple-shaped paperweights belongs to a
dedicated collector. Using books as pedestals
makes it easier to admire the many varieties on
display. All these apples tempt a trip to the
kitchen for a bite of the real thing.**

Celebratio

MOVABLE FEASTS. Do you eat in the same place all the time? Why not try another spot? Meals don't have to occur in the usual places.

On my birthday, I love having breakfast in bed, served to me by my husband and daughters. How wonderful it would be if we did this once a month instead of just once a year!

One of my girlfriends has a table for two in her bedroom by the window overlooking the garden. She and her husband read the paper and have coffee there every morning. Maybe there's a spot in your house where a little café table and chairs would fit.

Find a gazebo and eat with the scent of jasmine lingering in the air. In winter, have a Snow Ball outside. Set a table with lacy linens, drink cocoa from teacups, and eat coconut cake. Cover your knees with a chenille or cashmere throw and watch the snow fall.

Pop open a bottle of champagne by the fire and serve pâté on crusty bread. Toast it in the fire on long fireplace forks, or between the wires of an old-fashioned toasting rack.

TASTY BOUQUETS. I'm always looking for new ways to put some "teeth" into a simple bouquet of flowers, and this is one of the best. Surround the stems with whole fruits and vegetables in a

clear glass vase. Fill the vase with flowers and water as usual, and then add more layers of produce into the water, like bright orange kumquats, yellow lemons, little green apples, green beans, red peppers—any combination that looks appealing and can stand up to immersion without falling apart.

SEASONAL TASTES. When you decorate, food is a traditional way to signal the seasons. I have an old knurled basket that shuttles between the living room and the library. Pomegranates fill the basket at holidaytime, eggs say it's Easter, and oranges, lemons, and red peppers signal summer.

In the fall, I like to hang garlic and onion braids and a chili garland, and build apple pyramids using wire cones made especially for this purpose. In the winter, I put out a wheat stalk bundle for the birds.

Decorate with food where it's least expected. On a table outside your front door, a tureen filled with limes and pinecones can welcome guests as surely as a pine wreath.

THE ENTERTAINING SENSE. Taste is the entertaining sense. When we think of favorite parties we've loved (or given), our memory

> **Don't limit picnics to the warm-weather months. Eating outside can be a year-round adventure. On a day in crisp December, welcome winter with coconut cake and hot chocolate on the patio. Don't forget snowy linens to complete the occasion, and a throw to wrap around your shoulders.**

includes the foods and drinks we've enjoyed. . . .

The food that you serve, the presentation, the colors of the food, their smells, and the personality of the foods are all integral parts of designing for the sense of taste.

Food and drink often set the tone of an evening. When you walk into a friend's party, and you see petits fours and tea, you know it's going to be a very different event than if she were serving hamburgers and beer.

Certain foods create a sense of communion. Thanksgiving wonderfully marries its philosophical celebration with its foods. By all sitting around a table and sharing from a turkey, a large bowl of mashed potatoes, and all the trimmings, the ritual mirrors the themes of the occasion.

Chinese food is also wonderful in this way. By its nature, it bonds a group together by sharing from common serving dishes. On the more casual side, chili, roasting marshmallows, and barbecues create a bonding ambience.

Food presentation is such an underestimated element of design. Often the presentation not only gives a food its importance and beauty, but also betters the taste of the food. As with all design, the presentation of your food should reflect you—and your home.

It's the little things in a presentation that can make such a difference. The centerpiece presents a wonderful opportunity to create a focal point in a room. Tie in a color or theme that complements your food presentation. The arrangement and color of the foods on a plate often give a meal personality and dimension.

We recently took the kids out for a Sunday breakfast, and their pancakes were decorated with a "smiley face" made of whipped cream. The presentation not only made the food taste better, but it also paralleled the fun of the occasion.

What is the most glorious and symbolic of food presentations in American culture? The wedding cake. People don't remember the cake; they remember the presentation. Its size, its soft texture, and its color are all a metaphor of the ceremony. The cake is much more than a dessert. The wedding couple's cutting of the cake and handing it out to all their guests are glorious symbols of a wedding's communion.

There's the old saying, "Leave them with a good taste in their mouth." Bravo!

Today, a flower arrangement isn't just blossoms; what's in the water counts, too. The whole bouquet becomes a pillar for the senses—a smorgasbord of taste, sight, and smell. This shapely glass vase erupts with sunflowers, their throats tightly wrapped with a big bow of shimmering ribbon. Traditionally, this would be enough, but the vase is also filled with a colorful medley of red, green, and yellow peppers that look good enough to eat. The peppers are packed closely in the water, around the stems of the sunflowers. Marigolds and cockscomb are mounded above, filling in any gaps. To make your own showstopping bouquet, picture your arrangement from top to toe, and use every bit of space to make your statement. Fill the water with something interesting, and build as you go. Floral picks or toothpicks invisibly anchor things in place.

About the Tapestries

The enchanting Lady and the Unicorn tapestry is perhaps the most famous of all time. This magnificent work of art is made up of six individual panels. Each panel features a woman and a unicorn, and although the panels differ from each other, they are interrelated.

The complete tapestry, known as *La Dame à la Licorne*, now hangs in the Cluny Museum in Paris. Its beauty captures the timeless appeal of the senses, and how they have tantalized men and women through the ages. It also presents the moral dilemma of choosing between reason and desire.

The Lady and the Unicorn tapestry is rich in symbolism. The unicorn holds a position of importance in ancient, medieval, and Renaissance art. This proud and gentle creature was often shown on heraldic flags and banners. Each panel of the Lady and the Unicorn tapestry shows flags and banners bearing a French family's coat of arms.

While the tapestry can be enjoyed simply for its poetry and beauty, the figures in each panel held special significance in medieval times. Knowing these meanings makes the textiles even more interesting.

Is the unicorn real or imaginary? Some believe the unicorn was actually an Indian ass, or an animal known as the oryx, both of which had a single horn on their head. The noble unicorn seems to combine characteristics of the elephant, stag, bear, goat, and boar, and is depicted as being fierce in combat. The unicorn and the lion were often paired in medieval and early Renaissance art, carved furniture, and textiles. Sitting next to a lady, the unicorn symbolizes chastity. When the unicorn is shown with a man, it has all the virtues of a knight, at once gentle and courageous. The lion stands for bravery and compassion, and is said to be symbolic of Christ. The tapestry shows familiar animals like rabbits, dogs, birds, and lambs, and also unusual animals like the genet, a spotted mammal with a ringed tail that was popular in medieval times. Trees grow from the island in the center of each tapestry, and each panel has the millefleurs background of free-floating plants and flowers that is typical of medieval tapestries; flowers were often scattered on the ground on celebration days.

The Lady and the Unicorn tapestry has a counterpart in the Unicorn tapestries, which hang in The Cloisters museum in New York City's Fort Tryon Park, as part of the collection of the Metropolitan Museum of Art. These late-Gothic tapestries portray the Hunt of the Unicorn.

Much legend surrounds the enchanting Lady and the Unicorn tapestry, and through the ages, romantics have tried to interpret its message. Some believed it was woven for an imprisoned prince as a gift to his lover, or to represent a famous woman. We now know the tapestry was made during the late Middle

Ages, between 1484 and 1500. When footwear is shown, it can help date a tapestry, but as shoes are not visible in these panels, other indicators such as costumes and head coverings must be observed. From the coat of arms evident in the tapestry, we know it was woven for wealthy French merchant Jean Le Viste from the town of Lyon, but not, as was once supposed, to celebrate the 1513 marriage of Claude Le Viste; the ladies' costumes and the style of the tapestry seem to be earlier than that. The tapestry may have been commissioned to celebrate Le Viste's proud stature as head of his family or his appointment as president of the Court of Aids, an honor he received in 1489. By 1844, the tapestries were hanging on the walls of a French castle, and brought to the attention of the public by French author George Sand, who celebrated them in her novel *Jeanne*. (The tapestries also charmed French author Jean Cocteau and the lyric poet Rainer Maria Rilke, among others.) Some of the panels were eventually rescued from storage in Boussac Town Hall, and in 1883, the entire set went to the Cluny Museum in Paris. They are now displayed in a round hall specially designed to show them off.

It is astonishing that the Lady and the Unicorn tapestry has survived in such good condition. Tapestries were often treated roughly, rolled up and dragged from house to house by their owners. There are tales of majestic tapestries being used to wrap fruit trees during a cold snap, and of others being cut to fit around fireplaces on a wall, or rolled up and left lying in damp basements to be chewed by rats. It is rare to find a tapestry of this age in such fine condition, and the colors remain bright, although the entire set has been restored at various times, the panels' lower edges being especially vulnerable to decay and deterioration.

The Lady and the Unicorn tapestry is made of wool and silk. No one knows who painted the original designs for the Lady and the Unicorn tapestry, or who wove it. The millefleurs background suggests it may have been made in Brussels, one of the cities that specialized in this technique.

To begin a detailed tapestry like this one, a painter would do a preliminary sketch called a cartoon. The cartoon was delivered to a workroom, where a set of skilled weavers would copy the design, adding embellishments of their own to the basic drawing. Sometimes the weavers themselves did the cartoons, much to the consternation of the painters' guild.

Because of the way the looms were set up, the weavers worked sideways, and from the back of the tapestry. Knowing this, the detail of the tapestries becomes even more astonishing.

References:

Tapestry, by Barty Phillips (London: Phaidon Press, 1994).

The Unicorn Tapestries, by Margaret B. Freeman (New York: E.P. Dutton, 1976).

The Lady and the Unicorn, by Alain Erlande-Brandenburg (Paris: Réunion des Musées Nationaux, 1989).

Source Guide

CONTRIBUTING INTERIOR DESIGNERS

INTERIORS BY THOMAS CALLAWAY
2920 Nebraska Avenue
Santa Monica, CA 90404
310-828-1030

CATHERINE BAILLY DUNNE INTERIOR DESIGN
1349 Franklin Street
Santa Monica, CA 90404
310-454-4047

RAY INNER BUILDERS
Debbie Jones
253 26th Street
Santa Monica, CA 90402
310-476-1824

JANET LOHMAN INTERIOR DESIGN
10559 Rocca Place
Los Angeles, CA 90077
310-471-3955

PENELOPE BIANCHI MCCORMICK INTERIORS
1721 East Valley Road
Montecito, CA 93108
805-969-1110

LYNN PRIES DESIGN
12 Smithcliff
Laguna Beach, CA 93651
714-721-0356

ALLISON TAYLOR INTERIORS
5835 Varna Avenue
Van Nuys, CA 91401
818-783-9100

SOURCES

The following are a few of my favorite sources, many of which I've mentioned in the book. Please feel free to write or call them.

AGRARIA
Stanford Gibson Limited
1050 Howard Street
San Francisco, CA 94103
415-863-7700
Fax: 415-863-4626
Incense, potpourri, bath gel, soaps, drawer liners, candles. My favorite scent is Bitter Orange. Call to find a store near you.

ARCHIPELAGO BOTANICALS
1833 Lincoln Boulevard
Santa Monica, CA 90404
800-399-4994
Bath gels, body lotions, soaps, candles, votives. My favorite scent is Malaga Spice. Call to find a store near you.

BRENDA ANTIN
7319 Beverly Boulevard
Los Angeles, CA 90036
213-934-8451
Eclectic furniture from Europe for the house and garden.

DYANA BARRET
2712 Manhattan Avenue
Manhattan Beach, CA 90266
310-545-3268
Custom floral designs.

BELLEVIE COMPANY
1248 Sussex Turnpike, B10
Randolph, NJ 07869
201-895-3900
Fax: 201-895-5101
*Musical plates. They're great to hang
on your walls or for serving food.*

NANCY CORZINE
8747 Melrose Avenue
Los Angeles, CA 90069
310-652-4858
Furniture, fabrics, and silver accessories.

DESIGN WORKS, INC.
11 Hitching Post Road
Amherst, MA 01002
413-549-4763
Home Quick Planner.

DOLCE MIA DESIGN
1805-B Clement Avenue
Alameda, CA 94501
510-814-0440
*Great découpage picture frames
with flowers or fruit.*

F.I.R.E./L.T.D.
744 1/2 North La Cienega Boulevard
Los Angeles, CA 90069
310-652-9110
Fax: 310-652-6735
Lighting.

FRENCH COLLECTION
8687 Melrose Avenue
West Hollywood, CA 90069
310-652-7101
Fax: 310-652-3533
*Musical figurines, French tapestries,
and other delights from France.*

FRENCH DEPOT
1284 Coast Village Road
Montecito, CA 93108
805-969-1085
Antiques and accessories.

PIERRE FREY FABRICS
12 East 33rd Street, Eighth Floor
New York, NY 10016
212-213-3099
*My favorite brocades come from this charming fabric house.
All their fabrics have a wonderful French influence.*

CHUCK GARDNER
11362 Burnham Street
Los Angeles, CA 90049
310-476-0329
email: cgphotog@gte.net
Portrait photography.

GERBER HINGE COMPANY
647-649 North Fairfax Avenue
Los Angeles, CA 90036
213-655-6880
Fax: 213-655-8533
French decorative hardware.

HOULES
979 Third Avenue
New York, NY 10022
212-935-3900
*You can always find the perfect tassel or trim for your
upholstery or curtains. They also have great hardware.*

GINA B.
8672 Melrose Avenue
West Hollywood, CA 90069
310-652-4488
*Custom furniture. If you can dream it up,
they can make it.*

GIFT GARDEN ANTIQUES
AND COLLECTIBLES
15266 Antioch Street
Pacific Palisades, CA 90272
310-459-4114
Fax: 310-459-5016
Antiques and accessories.

HARMONY
360 Interlocken Boulevard, Suite 300
Broomfield, CO 80021
800-869-3446
Fax: 800-456-1139
*TurboSpa, Zen rain chimes, programmable
sound conditioner. Call for a catalog.*

THE HERB COTTAGE BY THE SEA
2093 Village Wood Road
Encinitas, CA 92024
760-634-5040
*They have great furniture oil. My favorite is Rosemary
and Roses. It enhances the wood and leaves a
wonderful herbal scent.*

IRENE HIROSE
P.O. Box 8554
Calabasas, CA 91372
818-222-6647
*Sachets, scented pillows, shoe stuffers. Call for a store
near you.*

HOLLYHOCK
214 North Larchmont Boulevard
Los Angeles, CA 90064
213-931-3400
Great books and antiques.

ILLUMINATIONS
384 Oyster Point Boulevard, #16
South San Francisco, CA 94080
1-800-CANDLES
*Candles, Candle of the Month Club, Neutralizer
Candle. Call for a catalog.*

JACOBS MUSICAL CHIMES
10579 Bloomfield Street
Los Alamitos, CA 90720
562-594-8790
800-627-5840
Fax: 562-598-0490
*Door chimes, desk chimes, and window chimes.
Call for a store near you.*

JAMES JENNINGS FURNITURE
8471 Melrose Avenue
West Hollywood, CA 90069
213-655-7823
Fax: 213-655-4388
Custom furniture.

MARY KAISER, LTD.
J. Elizabeth Sales Company
1933 South Broadway, Suite 660
Los Angeles, CA 90007
213-763-5734
800-429-9092
Fax: 213-763-5735
Ottomans and pillows. Call for a store near you.

KENT DESIGN & MANUFACTURING
3522 Lousma Drive SE
Grand Rapids, MI 49548
616-243-7555
Woven wire grilles.

KNEEDLER-FAUCHERE
8687 Melrose Avenue
Los Angeles, CA 90069
310-855-1313
*Updated traditional furniture and my
favorite tapestry pillows.*

LEMON GRASS
367 West Broadway
New York, NY 10013
212-343-0900
*Tactile soaps. My two favorite soaps are
Orange Peel and Poppy Seed.*

MARK LOHMAN PHOTOGRAPHY
1021 South Fairfax Avenue
Los Angeles, CA 90019
213-933-3359

MELROSE HOUSE
8454 Melrose Place
Los Angeles, CA 90069
213-651-2202
Furniture and accessories.

MIDSUMMER COMMON
1123 Montana Avenue
Santa Monica, CA 90403
310-458-0081
Pillows and quilts.

MULLIGANS
8157 Sunset Boulevard
Los Angeles, CA 90067
213-650-8660
Great painted furniture and accessories.

OAKMONT
8687 Melrose Avenue
Los Angeles, CA 90069
310-659-1423
Great French and English fabrics.
*They sell Designers' Guild fabric.
One of my favorites is Salsa.*

PALMETTO
1034 Montana Avenue
Santa Monica, CA 90403
310-395-6687
Tactile soaps.

POINDEXTER'S AUDIO-VIDEO ENVIRONMENTS
2918 Santa Monica Boulevard
Santa Monica, CA 90404
310-829-1102
Fax: 310-315-2878
www.poindexters.com
*Audio/video equipment. Call the Web site for
waterproof speakers for your bathroom.*

RICHARD MARSHALL FLOORING
12824 Cerise Avenue
Hawthorne, CA 90250
310-644-0992
Hardwood flooring.

RAMBOUILLET TAPESTRIES
Dallas Market Center
2050 Stemmons Freeway, Suite 11074
P.O. Box 58345
Dallas, TX 75258
800-323-7422
*French decorative arts. You may purchase reproductions
of the Unicorn tapestries through this supplier.*

ROOM WITH A VIEW
1600 Montana
Santa Monica, CA 90403
310-998-5858
Great linens and gift items.

ANN SACKS TILE & STONE
Sheri Hirschfeld
8483 Melrose Avenue
West Hollywood, CA 90069
213-658-8884
*Tile and stone. Ask about their original
New York pavers. They're great.*

SENTIMENTO
306 East 61st Street
New York, NY 10022
212-750-3111
*There's always something exciting to discover
here in the way of antique furniture or accessories.*

SOOLIP PAPERIE & PRESS
8646 Melrose Avenue
West Hollywood, CA 90069
310-360-0545
Fax: 310-360-0548
*Scented inks and desk accessories. My favorite
scented ink is Rose!*

STARK CARPET CORPORATION
8687 Melrose Avenue
Los Angeles, CA 90069
310-657-8275
Fax: 310-657-8634
Carpet and floor coverings.

TERRA COTTA
11922 San Vincente
Los Angeles, CA 90049
310-826-7878
Wonderful antiques and gift items.

WATER ART
2432 West Glenoaks Avenue
Anaheim, CA 92801
714-527-5080
Fax: 714-527-2796
Tabletop fountains.

WILLIAM A. KARGES FINE ART
Whitney Ganz, Director
9001 Melrose Avenue
Los Angeles, CA 90069
310-276-8551
www.kargesfineart.com
Fine art.

WORLDS AWAY
397 Front Street
Memphis, TN 38103
901-529-0844
Fax: 901-527-3406
*Tole lamps, urns, trays, and lanterns. I use the
lanterns for entertaining in the evening. Call for a
store near you.*

YOMA TEXTILES
580 Broadway, #1209
New York, NY 10012
212-431-4794
*This fabric collection is unique because it incorporates
textures, scale, and pattern with touches of Asian influence.
My favorite is Savanna, a great cotton velvet in wonderful
colors.*

Index

About the Author

CATHERINE BAILLY DUNNE'S award-winning interior designs have transformed multimillion-dollar homes, estates, and offices from Beverly Hills to New York. She has captivated audiences on numerous national television shows, in magazines and newspapers, and on the Internet and radio programs all around the globe. She was educated at the premier university of interior design, Parsons School of Design in New York, and has studied in Paris and Los Angeles. She lives with her husband and two daughters in Pacific Palisades, California.

About the Photographer

MARK LOHMAN is a freelance photographer who specializes in interiors, architecture, and travel. His work has appeared in *Country Living, Architectural Record, Better Homes and Gardens, House Beautiful*, and *Country Homes*. He lives with his wife and children in Los Angeles, California.